This is a timeless and impor g with his wife, Harvey, and son, B ɔny to the work that God will do w ɡreatest challenges. At a time when ʜ of the country and culture are being consumed and degraded by injustice, addiction, and failure, *Daddy, Why Are You Going To Jail?* tells the amazing tale of how the Lord took a family from a challenging low point to a position of true freedom and peace. Our failure is powerful fuel. This book is a must read for anyone who wonders what good might come from the trials they are now facing. Stephen Lawson gives us a glimpse of the supernatural and redemptive power of God. On behalf of those who still work for Prison Fellowship, the wonderful ministry in which Stephen Lawson and his family participated, we are so thankful to share in the telling of this story.

—*Craig DeRoche, Senior Vice President,*
*Advocacy & Public Policy, Prison Fellowship*

This second edition of *Daddy, Why Are You Going To Jail?* is truly a divine appointment for any reader. It is not a sugar-coated story of a man's life being transformed by Christ but a very real story of life's ups and downs even after one has become a Christian. It is also a vital read for anyone sentenced to prison or in the process of re-entering society. Stephen once asked the question: "I wonder how Zacchaeus lived the rest of his life after that treetop experience?" He found the answer to that question and also discovered the "rest of the story" by his, Harvey's, and Blake's journey toward the ancient Eastern Orthodox faith that Jesus gave to His apostles, and they in turn passed the story on to their disciples and so on through the centuries. May each reader find their journey enriched and blessed through this wonderful book.

—*Fr. Stephen Powley, Executive Director,*
*Orthodox Christian Prison Ministry*

Stephen, Harvey, and Blake share an amazing story of captivity and freedom! Personally, I have an active prison ministry in Georgia. I see the difficulties of prison time both for the prisoners and for their families. One of the biggest issues those incarcerated face is being forgotten by others. God's grace is the power to deliver people from spiritual, emotional, and physical captivity. Jesus came to set us free. He said, "He that the Son sets free is free indeed." This wonderful book will fill you with great joy and peace as you share their story of freedom in Christ.

—*Dr. David Cooper, Lead Pastor,*
*Mount Paran Church, Atlanta, Georgia*

Knowing the Lawsons for over 30 years, I have always been struck by how utterly non-religious the three of them are, while being purely sold out to God. They are a breath of fresh air. Their faith came through tragic human failure. Their punishment was severe, more from the abandonment of friends and the struggle to make it financially than from the actual incarceration. Then the only real Friend they had walked them out of their shame and into a life of joy and service. Deeply in love with each other, Harvey not only stayed with her husband but, along with Blake, partnered with Steve in his redemption. What a page turner; what a faith-building read this is.

—*Sarah Lanier, author,* Foreign to Familiar:
A Guide to Hot—and Cold—Climate Cultures

I will be giving *Daddy, Why Are You Going to Jail?* to three different sets of friends. For those who are uncertain about the God of the Bible, I'll give it knowing that as they read they will hear an honest and compelling account of God's liberating grace. For my Evangelical friends, this book opens us to the journey of faith in which Christ is loved even as he guides a family into a new way of being Christian. Finally, for the Eastern Orthodox in my circle, I believe this book will help them better understand their Protestant friends, while also confirming the deep power manifested in the historic faith. I found myself so taken with the story that I was up reading it late into the night, wanting to learn what would happen. How glad I am that Stephen, Harvey, and Blake told us the rest of the story.

—*The Rev. Dr. Gregory C. Faulkner, Senior Pastor, Trinity Presbyterian Church, Cherry Hill, New Jersey*

Karen and I have known Stephen and Harvey Lawson and their son, Blake, for over thirty-five years. We've shared lunches, dinners, and some short road trips over the years. Their story is one of redemption and restoration. They tell of a loving and merciful God who responded and lifted them above the dire circumstances of an eight-year prison sentence. The Lord restored and redeemed their lives, allowing them to go from riches to rags to the true riches that only a relationship with Jesus Christ can afford.

—*Kenneth Boa, PhD, DPhil, President, Reflections Ministries and Omnibus Media*

This is a book that springs from the heart, a heart deeply affected by God's Love and Mercy. Sometimes it takes our own fall to make us realize that the glittering things of the world cannot be the goal of our lives. Stephen Lawson wrote this book at a time when he had realized how far he had fallen, but also how much God's Love had lifted him up and held him and his family in the midst of adversity. His wife, Harvey, and their son, Blake, were encouraged to offer a second edition of the original book. Stephen and Harvey wrote the rest of the story—the next thirty-four years that they include in this new book. Their desire is to share God's Love and Mercy with those who might be in the midst of their own adversity. The purpose of the book is to reassure people that God is always there to help us navigate the difficult circumstances of life. All we need to do is turn to Him!

—*Fr. Panayiotis Papageorgiou, PhD, Presiding Protopresbyter, Holy Transfiguration Greek Orthodox Church, Marietta, Georgia*

# DADDY,
## WHY ARE YOU
## GOING TO JAIL?

To Eva and Steve,
you are a blessing and
May the Lord continue to bless you!

Harvey Sampson

Isa 12:4-5

You two are fantastic and
I am so happy that I know
you. So when are we coming over
for dinner?

Blake

SECOND EDITION

# DADDY, WHY ARE YOU GOING TO JAIL?

*The True Story of a Father's Descent into White-Collar Crime and* **His Amazing Restoration**

## STEPHEN P. LAWSON, ELYSE HARVEY LAWSON, AND BLAKE S. LAWSON

credo
house publishers

Published in the United States by Credo House Publishers,
a division of Credo Communications, LLC, Grand Rapids, Michigan
credohousepublishers.com

Unless otherwise indicated, Scripture quotations are taken from the
Holy Bible, New International Version®, NIV®. Copyright © 1973,
1978, 1984, 2011 by Biblica, Inc.™ Used by permission of Zondervan.
All rights reserved worldwide. www.zondervan.com. The "NIV" and
"New International Version" are trademarks registered in the United
States Patent and Trademark Office by Biblica, Inc.™

ISBN 978-1-625861-23-8

Cover and interior design by Frank Gutbrod
Editing by Amy Leskowski

Many of the names in this story have been changed in order to protect
privacy. Each name change is indicated by an asterisk (*) after its first
occurrence.

*Printed in the United States of America*
Second Edition

This book tells of the faithfulness, mercy, and love of God. It also tells of the faithfulness, mercy, and love of my best friend, sister in Christ, wife, and the nicest person I have ever known—Elyse Harvey Lawson. My earnest prayer is that our son, Blake, might someday be blessed enough to marry as well as I have.

Many others have contributed greatly in blessing our lives. You are known and appreciated by us and by our Lord. To Harvey, Blake, and all of you, this book is lovingly dedicated.

*"May the* Lord *repay you for what you have done. May you be richly rewarded by the* Lord*, the God of Israel, under whose wings you have come to take refuge."*
Ruth 2:12

Stephen P. Lawson 1992

# DEDICATION 2019

While I was rereading the original book and working with my book editor on the new edition I marveled once again at the astonishing grace we were extended. It is not that I had ever forgotten, but now at age 76 so much of life has transpired that it was just tucked away in my memory. I continue to be thankful for each person and their unique contributions and friendship and most especially for the mercy and love of God.

To Patti and Don Patterson who showed the love of Christ in more ways than I can ever relate along with the late Grace Kinser and the Friday morning men's prayer group, I dedicate this work to you. To the McHenry family who insisted on paying Blake's tuition when we could not, and to Deen Day Smith who started all this rolling through her generous support of Stephen's very lengthy original manuscript when they agreed he needed a book editor. Joanne and Homer stood by us when our world was falling apart. There are more, many more, but I can't begin to include all the wonderful acts of kindness and generous hearts as there aren't enough pages in this book to list everyone who prayed and encouraged us, but you are most certainly known by God. Your bounty and grace were overwhelming, and we are eternally grateful.

I lovingly dedicate this book to all those who love the Lord, believe His Word, and through Him showed their love to us. To God—all praise, honor, thanksgiving, and glory are yours.

*Elyse Harvey Lawson and Blake S. Lawson*
*2019*

# CONTENTS

## PART 2  THE REST OF THE STORY

# FOREWORD TO THE FIRST EDITION

With the recent twentieth anniversary of the Watergate break-in, I have been barraged with media requests and then interviewers' questions: As a White House conspirator, what was I thinking? Did I set out to break the law? No. One seemingly insignificant questionable decision led to another until a federal prosecutor was asking big questions about a cover-up and I had little defense.

As the owner and president of a prominent Atlanta real estate investment firm, Steve Lawson let one rationalized shady "gamble" build on another until his world fell apart. Like thousands of other "white-collar criminals," he never suspected that someday he would plead guilty—before an earthly judge and, more important, before a heavenly Judge.

Sitting in the federal courtroom dock, Steve received no mercy from the bench—a stiff term in a federal prison camp.

But on his knees before his Maker, he found life-transforming power to face life and turn his back on plans for suicide; he found forgiveness and peace with God that would carry him through the trauma of incarceration.

I know what that word means for a man or woman who has a family. You're willing to pay the consequences for your own wrongdoing, but you can hardly bear the pain of knowing the hardship your actions have brought on your spouse, your children, your parents.

For offenders married when they enter prison, statistics are disheartening. Eighty-five percent of those prisoners will not have a spouse to return home to. Then another ten percent of the marriages will not survive the first few years after the prisoner's release; the transition places too much stress on the family bond.

*Daddy, Why Are You Going to Jail?* is a book about a family's ability to walk forward into and through forgiveness. By the grace of God, Steve and his wife, Harvey, and their son, Blake, weathered the storm, choosing to cling to each other and to the God of second chances.

I first met Steve in 1980 when he was furloughed from the prison camp in Fort Walton Beach, Florida, to attend an intensive two-week Prison Fellowship seminar designed to disciple and give leadership skills to believers who would return to prison and minister to fellow inmates—the church behind bars.

At the closing "graduation," Steve's very countenance as he stood to speak briefly before the packed church was a testimony to God's work in and through him. For a time after his release he directed our Prison Fellowship work in the state of Georgia. He, like me, could not easily walk away from the needs so evident in the lives of prisoners, ex-prisoners, and their families.

Steve and Harvey came to know God through the witness of friends and the piercing power of the two-edged Word of God. May the Holy Spirit use Steve's witness in these pages to touch the hearts of readers seeking a reason to live or a reason to forgive, even when bad choices—yours or someone else's—have set your life in a tailspin.

*Chuck Colson, Chairman*
*Prison Fellowship*

# PREFACE

As this witness of my Lord and Savior Jesus Christ unfolds, it is my prayer it will tell of a life that has made a moral amendment in Jesus—the witness of a Jew who had his faith grow after crying out in a last desperate act of hope. My witness in Jesus Christ relates:

- Every adversity hides a beautiful possibility!
- A person is able to be an important part of God's plan for that day!
- The Lord gives us dominion over our every limitation!
- Troubles can become triumphs!
- One can be in prison but respond rightly as one who has hope!
- One is able to forgive and feel forgiven!
- Delay doesn't mean denial—especially of his love!

So in this book I open our lives to you with a great deal of enthusiasm because I am excited to share the faithfulness of a Lord who has dealt lovingly, with grace and mercy.

*Stephen P. Lawson*
*Atlanta, Georgia*
*1992*

# ACKNOWLEDGMENTS 1992

For the most part, first-time authors without public name recognition have a difficult time getting published. My agent, Joyce Farrell, believed this autobiography needed to be shared and worked diligently in presenting the manuscript to various publishing houses. All the while she was a source of great encouragement to me.

Ramona Cramer Tucker, Director of Editorial Services, at Harold Shaw Publishers was a pleasure to work with. Her belief in this manuscript was always heartening, and the talent and time she shared so liberally has allowed this story to be everything it was intended to be.

To both of these ladies, my family joins me in thanking you.

# ACKNOWLEDGEMENTS 2019

I n 2019 Harvey wishes to recognize and thank Peter Lundell and Tim Beals. Introduced to Peter Lundell through Cec Murphy, who is known and loved by Christian writers, Peter is a talented author, writer, and pastor; but his editorial gifts were just what I needed—a better word or phrase and his ability to cut superfluous paragraphs. Tim Beals, the founder and publisher of Credo House Publishers, is a fine, patient gentleman with a terrific publishing background. Both men were wonderful to work with and made this complicated journey pleasurable. I will always be thankful to them and for them.

Blake and I also wish to recognize our *Book Angels,* without whom this current book would not be a reality. It is with a full heart and unending gratitude that we acknowledge their donations, prayers, and encouragement. We launched a GoFundMe campaign and video in early 2018 to raise the money to republish the original book and add the new Part 2. Proceeds from the sale of the book will be shared between Angel Tree, a Prison Fellowship ministry, and Orthodox Christian Prison Ministry. We established a non-profit corporation and 501 (3)(c) in the name of the book, *Daddy, Why Are You Going to Jail?*

To God be the glory; may each of you be blessed both now and always!

Ida Bell
Evelyn Bilson
George Boudouris
Brayfield Productions
Margaret Ann and Frank Briggs
Carolyn F. Brown
Paule Chalmers
Michelle and Scott Davidson
Marty Driscoll
Merrill Ellis
Dalby and Don Etheridge
Elaine and Steve Franklin
Joel Freeman
Niki and Larry Gess
Lee and Jenny Hadbavny
Sally and John Howard
Jim Johnson
Vesta and David Jones
Beverly and Mel Koontz
Pat Koutouzis
Sarah Lanier
Mary and Bob McCauley
Ioanna Michaels

Lana Moye
Chatham Murray
Ryan Oliver
Presbytera Catherine and Fr. Panayiotis Papageorgiou
Deloris and Chuck Perkins
Sue and Bob Perkins
Kay Pound
Vicki Proano
Diane Reese
Andrea Shaparenko
Kathy Shoji
Carol Silva
Herb and Nancy Raffa Sodel Fund
Marion Spence
Christel M. Stokes
Dee and George Sullivan
Janice and Chuck Sutherland
Van Waddy
Braden Weber
Libba Wight
Joanne Wright
Anne Young

# PART 1
# THE STORY

# Chapter 1

# GOOD-BYE, MY LITTLE BOY

Friday morning, March 2, 1979, started like any other day. The alarm buzzed at 6 a.m.

Harvey and I awoke at once. Our eyes met and said it all: Is this really happening? Has the day really arrived—this day we've dreaded?

The last forty-five days had not prepared us for this moment. I had some knowledge of child psychology, but I could see how impossible it was going to be to put what little I knew into practice. How was I going to look at my son, Blake, and tell him what I had to say? Would the words even come out?

My wife, Harvey, tied the cloth belt to her robe, padded over to where I stood, and hugged me. "Oh, God," she whispered with tears in her throat, "Please be with Stephen and me. This is so tough. If we can make it for the next hour, there won't be anything too hard to handle."

She started to walk away, but I reached to pull her close again. "Harvey, I love you so much. Honey, do you really understand that I'm another person now and how sorry I am for . . ." I couldn't finish, but she knew what I meant.

"I know," she replied. "It's just that right now it doesn't make things any easier. Please, honey, I need to go to the kitchen. Can you get Blake dressed and ready for breakfast?"

Blake's ride to school was due in forty-five minutes. Harvey and I had agreed that we needed the extra fifteen minutes to break the news to him.

How do you tell the joy of your heart that you're going to prison? How is it possible to express how awful you feel and at the same time assure your son that everything will be okay—someday?

In recent weeks I had gone to Blake's room every evening after he'd fallen asleep and sat on the bed next to him. I would touch my beautiful child's face or stroke his hair. He was asleep and at peace. He knew nothing of how drastically his life was about to change. Most evenings I whispered to him the things that were on my heart, knowing he couldn't hear, much less understand.

"I'm sorry, son." The words would struggle out as tears ran down my face. "Your mom and I waited to have a family for a long time—until everything was just right—and now look what I've done."

His breathing was regular and deep, the soft eyelashes still against his cheeks. The words kept spilling out, as much a prayer as an explanation. "You didn't ask to be born. You didn't count on this kind of heartbreak. I hope you won't be too scared over this and that you'll still be able to love and forgive me. If I knew you couldn't forgive me, son, I'd honestly rather die."

Each night, while putting my hand on top of Blake's head, I would talk to my Father: God, I don't even know how to pray for him, but I leave Blake with you and ask you to bless him in all ways, to protect him, and to love him through the tough times ahead. Oh, God, please don't let my failures become stumbling blocks in his young life.

Later in bed—long after the lights were turned off and I could hear Harvey breathing rhythmically in sleep—I would pray for her in the stillness of the night. Life would be rough for her. Besides the burden of single parenting, there were the finances; I had no idea how she would make ends meet without any income from me.

I also prayed a lot for myself; I didn't know how I would survive eight years in prison.

Christian friends and members of various prayer groups around Atlanta knew of my upcoming incarceration, and several attempted to give me encouragement: "Steve, what a wonderful ministry you can have there," or, "What a marvelous opportunity to get deeper into the Word." I couldn't help but think, somewhat facetiously, that if it weren't for the marvelous opportunities awaiting me in prison, I'd really rather not go!

As each day passed and the commitment date loomed closer, the dark realities hit me with greater and greater force. My prayers for my son intensified as I fought panic. *Let him understand and not resent me. Don't allow him to feel abandoned . . . or to think that any of this could somehow be his fault.*

We had been advised on our dealings with Blake by a close friend, Liz,* who had several degrees in psychology and counseling. She said we must be completely honest with Blake. We agreed, as it would be difficult to convince even a five-year-old that his father would be out of town on business for a while—and stay away until he was nearly fourteen. Even if we weren't truthful, his classmates would be. I wanted the news to come from me. That much I could do for him, as little as it seemed to be.

Liz also stressed that it would be important for Blake to realize that I was going to a "camp" for daddies who had made mistakes rather than a maximum-security prison like Blake had sometimes seen on television. "You must help him realize that you did not commit a violent crime," Liz emphasized. "And once he visits you he will feel better after seeing the environment. At this age, Blake has no perception of time. If you tell him you'll be leaving in forty-five days, he'll have no idea of when that is. It would be silly—even cruel—to put him under any strain for that period of time. Better to prepare him by saying you will have to be leaving for a long time, sometime soon. Then, when you finally break the news, attempt to keep it as light as possible."

*As light as possible?* That would be the hardest part—to make it appear that everything would be all right while I crumbled inside. Prayer or no prayer, the pain of my coming separation from those I loved most was ever present.

I decided to make the last days with Blake a time filled with good memories, closeness, and companionship. I hoped that the better part of eight years away would not wipe out special times we had always experienced together. "Blake, how would you like to take one of your dad's best piggyback rides?"

"Okay, Daddy, but don't move too fast until I get a good hold." He climbed up while I rested swaybacked on all fours. "Giddy up, horse!" he shouted gleefully.

I moved around the living room, occasionally bucking, speeding up, and slowing down. All the while my heart was breaking.

"Oh my, this old horse is getting tired. I think I'll stop over here and take a nap," I said softly.

"Be careful! I don't want to fall off!"

I slid to the carpet and lay on my stomach while Blake toppled off, then I rolled over to smother him in hugs and kisses while he squealed with delight.

"Blake, you know pretty soon Daddy is going to have to go away for a long time. I'm sure going to miss you. Are you going to miss me too?"

"Uh-huh. I'll lift my arm up, and you see if you can tickle me under my arm before I put it down, okay?"

Obviously, he had heard me but had no idea what the words meant. The arm went up, his face gleaming with anticipation of how wonderful his newly made-up game would be. He was a bundle of little-boy energy in his red corduroy jumpsuit with the yellow Pooh Bear on the front. I tickled him, and the most beautiful laughter in the world filled the room.

Lord, thank you for loving my little boy even more than I do. I hold you to your promise to never leave or forsake us—or allow us to go through more than we can endure.

We were finally able to make Blake aware that on the following Friday his mom and I would go to Florida. The time had come to tell him that only his mom was making it round-trip. Friday arrived; the day we dreaded. Today is the day to tell Blake.

I went into Blake's room and began the regular wake-up routine. He lay on his stomach fast asleep.

"Good morning!" I called cheerfully as I rubbed his back and patted his rump through the blanket. "It's time to get up."

"Can I sleep a little longer?" he asked sleepily, as he did every morning, eyes still closed.

"You know it's a school day, and the car pool will pick you up in a little while. Come on. Up and at 'em."

Before long he was dressed and fed. Now wide awake, he played in his room, putting together the last pieces to a Donald Duck jigsaw puzzle.

Harvey and I walked into the room together. I sat on Blake's bed while Harvey stood, leaning on the dresser for support. I took a deep breath.

"Honey, put the puzzle down and come here for a minute. There's something Daddy has to tell you."

Blake put the last piece of the puzzle into place. Then he crossed the room and plopped down next to me on the bed, his short legs dangling a foot or so from the carpet.

*He's so young. How in the world can I help him understand this?* I agonized. He looked up at me. People have always said Blake looks a lot like me, but as I stared at him, he reminded me more of his mother, his eyes bluer than ever, the lashes incredibly long.

"What do you want to tell me?" he asked brightly. "Is it a surprise?"

"Do you remember how Daddy has said many times that he might have to go away for a *lonnng* time?"

"Yes." He nodded, his eyes full of questions.

"Well, Daddy is going to drive to a place in Florida today and—"

"Oh, boy! Can I go, too? Please, Daddy?" he squealed with delight. He jumped off the bed and faced me, all smiles. "When are we going to go? What will we do in Florida?"

"Son, wait a minute. Sit back up here next to me on the bed."

As Blake climbed up on the bed again, I stole my first glance at Harvey. I had never seen so much sorrow in her face. Her keen blue eyes watered, and her drawn features seemed transfixed in watching a heartbreaking event. I knew how powerless she felt. Our eyes met. She bit her lip and slowly shook her head.

I turned back to Blake, feeling like I couldn't breathe. My next statement would change his world. "Daddy is going to drive to a place in Florida today, with Mommy and Liz." I spoke quickly, compulsively, not inviting interruptions. "I'll have to stay there a long time, but I want you to know that I love you and Mommy with all my heart and that I'm going to be counting the days until I can come home again so we can be a family."

His eyes, like mine, filled with tears. "Daddy, don't go—"

"Son, I don't want to go, but I have to."

"Why?"

"Daddy made a . . . mistake in business and broke the law. You know how Daddy has to punish you when you're naughty?"

He nodded solemnly.

"Well, it's the same thing when you're grown up—even when you're a daddy. I did some things that were wrong

. . . very wrong . . . so I went to court where a judge told me I had to go to a place called a work camp, along with other daddies who have made mistakes. I'll have to stay there a long time."

"No!" he cried, the tears gushing down his face now. "Don't go, Daddy! Tell him I don't want you to go!"

I knew that the ocean of tears I had held back all those times we played couldn't be stayed now for more than another sixty seconds. "Boy, I'm going to miss you and Mommy," I finished, in a vain effort to keep my voice light. "What did you do wrong?" Blake asked through his tears.

How could I possibly explain security violations and mail fraud to him? "It's hard for me to explain to you right now," I said, haltingly. "But I didn't *hurt* anybody, and it isn't like anything you see on TV police programs. I've never done anything like that. Someday when you're older and you can understand better, I'll tell you all about it."

Blake slid to the floor and planted himself in front of me, looking up with glistening eyes. "You can tell me *now*. I'm a big boy. I'm five years old, you know."

I pulled him close so that I wouldn't have to look into his eyes anymore. The sobs started. They began in my stomach, worked themselves into my throat, and wrenched out of my mouth in sounds I'd never heard before. My body convulsed, but I could not allow myself to give in.

Harvey came to my rescue with marvelous voice control. "Everything will be fine. We are a family, and we love one another." She got on her knees and took Blake's two hands in her own, gazing deeply into his eyes. "Blake, darling, everything is going to be okay. Daddy and I both love you, and Daddy and I love each other."

"But I don't want him to go," he sobbed.

"I know—I don't either. But we'll visit him often. As a matter of fact, how would you like to go to Florida with me in about two weeks to visit him?"

"Okay. But I still don't want him to go."

She embraced him. "I know." Her blue eyes locked with mine. This hadn't gone well, but somehow it was over. We had told him, and he knew. We didn't have to dread the event anymore.

I knelt down beside them, tears still streaming down my face. "I guess I'm the most blessed person in the world to have a family like you guys." I smiled as best I could. "You know, the amount of time I have to spend away won't compare to all the years we'll have together as a family when this is all over. I love you, Blake, and I'm very proud of you."

A horn sounded from the driveway. Blake's ride with three other children his age waited for him.

"Of all mornings to be early!" I said with manufactured cheeriness. Harvey dried her tears and blotted Blake's face so she could take him downstairs.

As they were going out the front door, Blake turned and bolted back up the stairs to me. I picked him up and hugged him, feeling his smooth cheek against mine.

"I love you, Daddy."

"I love you too, son. Be Dad's best boy and listen to your mother while I'm gone. Promise?"

"I promise."

"I'm going to write you every day, so watch for the mail. I'm even going to address the envelopes to *you*." I hoped that the forced smile and upbeat voice were convincing.

Harvey and Blake went downstairs while I walked over to the window and watched. After a half minute of small talk with Harvey, the driver pulled out. I watched the car disappear around the bend on Peachtree Road. By then, Harvey had returned. She draped her arm across my back.

There was nothing to say, so we stood quietly for a few moments. I had just watched half my heart leave, and I wasn't at all sure what was going on inside my son. I couldn't move away from the window.

"I only wish I could be Blake for the next hour or so," I murmured. "Then I'd know exactly what is going through his mind. It would help us know what to do to make it easier for him somehow."

Harvey's arm dropped to my waist, and I turned, squeezing her close to me.

"Heavenly Father," she prayed, "Stephen and I pray that any trauma, bitterness, or lack of understanding Blake might feel will be openly expressed and in no way suppressed. Father, give me wisdom and love to deal with Blake during these days and years ahead. Show me what he needs, and give me the ability to deal with it. But, Lord, please be with Blake now and send guardian angels to give him comfort. Let him know that we are a blessed family who love each other but most of all love you."

Shortly afterward, Liz arrived. We packed the car, and I asked them to remain downstairs while I took one last private tour of our apartment. Slowly I passed from room to room, looking at objects I particularly loved, remembering each occasion they represented.

I walked into the living room and was drawn to the formal portrait of my father. Dad had died fourteen years earlier. When he was alive, I considered him a friend as well as my father. "How I wish you were here today, Dad," I said under my breath. Then I checked myself. "It's probably better this way, though. Why live to the age you would be now, only to have this grief kill you?"

My father's life had been a difficult one. At one time he had been a wealthy man and had the respect, perhaps even envy, of many. Then his business had failed. He lost money, people's respect, and his good-time friends. Dad also lost his wife, even though they existed together until he died.

Mom had never recovered from the pressure and the strain. She held considerable bitterness toward many people, including Dad. In the photograph I held in my hands, Dad looked at peace. As my eyes rested on his, it was as though he had, for the moment, come alive. I experienced a deep love and understanding from him that I had never known before.

The tears flowed openly. "Dad, forgive me for the shame I've brought to the Lawson name," I whispered. "I really loved you, but because of the way things were at home, I guess I never got around to telling you."

I sat down on the sofa with a heavy heart and caved in with sobs again. This pain seemed like it would go on forever. But it seemed important to continue this talk I was having with Dad. I cradled his picture in one hand. In the quietness of the room, it was as though he lived and could hear everything I said through my sobs.

"Dad, I have a son now, whom you never got to meet. He's a fine boy. You would have liked him, and I would have loved for you to be his grandfather." I sat still while the hurricane rocked inside me. "Where is all this going to end, Dad? I've lost my money, the same as you. My old friends have disappeared, just like yours did."

Then, for some moments, I spoke to my heavenly Father, begging him not to allow Blake to be the victim of a victim the way I had been. *Break this chain. Condition his little heart not to feel resentment toward me and to love me in spite of the bad decisions I've made,* I prayed, for God's ears alone.

I turned back to Dad's picture. "The most important thing in my life right now is for Blake to be able to forgive me—and I have a lot more in my life to be forgiven for than you did." Suddenly, for the first time in my life, I knew why I had wrestled so much with my relationship with my dad. "I never really forgave you," I said. No one in our family had ever said "I'm sorry" for anything, and no one had ever spoken words of forgiveness. Sorrowfully, I began to forgive my father—for the times he hadn't been there, for not being interested enough in my life, for never expressing pride in my accomplishments. I forgave him for not standing his ground with my mother, for allowing her anger to control our household. One by one, the grievances came to mind, and I said, "Dad, I forgive you." Then I saw with startling clarity the ways in which I had wronged him and my mother. With each remembrance, I asked, "Please forgive *me.*"

Finally, I wiped my face. I was cleansed. Something wonderful had just taken place; I knew that God had been—was still—present in the room. I returned Dad's picture to its place and picked up a picture of Harvey and me taken at the Southampton Princess Hotel in Bermuda. What a happy time we'd had. Would we ever know times like that again? Was there a way that one could pick up the pieces and start new dreams? Would the long years away wear out Harvey's resolve and love for me? Would we still be a family when it was all over, as we'd both promised our son? Even if Harvey didn't leave me, would our relationship become like that of my parents?

I thrust away the dark doubts, for I knew that Harvey's and my life together was quite different from what my parents' had been. God had already freed me from an infinitely harsher—if invisible—prison. Surely he would walk with us both during our years of confinement. Harvey serving her sentence, me serving mine.

I drank in every detail of my home, wondering how many treasured possessions would have to be sold off for pennies on the dollar so that Harvey could put food on the table. So many things truly were in God's hands now; every power had been stripped from me.

*Lord, this is too much for me to handle. I can't bear it without your help.* With that final cry for assistance, I clapped my hands together in much the same way football players do when a huddle is broken. I took a last look around and then walked out the door.

Harvey would later recall, "I know the Lord says that we should only concern ourselves with the events of today, since tomorrow has enough worries of its own. At that awful moment it was easy to do the scriptural thing. The present was so painful and the future so bleak and uncertain that I couldn't contemplate trying to think past today. Tomorrow seemed years away. I was like a piece of driftwood caught in a current of a turbulent river, along for the ride. I didn't ask to be thrown into the river; I was truly an innocent victim of Stephen's past actions. Would Blake and I be able to continue to live in our residence? Would I have to move in with my mother or Aunt Francine? How long would Stephen be away? What in the world was going to become of us? My questions and concerns were endless."

# Chapter 2

# A CHANGE OF ADDRESS

Perhaps no other place is as lovely as Atlanta in March, as it heralds the beginning of spring. Jonquils, crocuses, dogwood trees, and azalea bushes awaken after a winter's rest and bloom in profusion. And that day no one appreciated them more than I did. As we drove through Atlanta, heading south, I devoured all the sights, especially our immediate neighborhood. I wanted to remember everything in vivid detail; years would pass before I would ever see it again.

We drove most of the seven hours with little conversation. Our thoughts centered on Blake, yet we had nothing new to say. So we sat with our private thoughts and didn't try to force conversation.

Because of Liz's generous offer, we stayed at a beautiful Destin, Florida, condo that overlooked a golf course. We bought shrimp at a local fish market for our evening meal and cooked it ourselves. We wanted to be close to the phone. We had prearranged to call Blake at 7:30 p.m. to find out how he was handling my being gone. And on our part we wanted to furnish an upbeat, positive report.

For that weekend, we had left Blake with friends of ours whose children Blake enjoyed. We wanted to believe he was having a wonderful time. We had been careful not to mention the word "prison," saying "work camp" instead. We decided that when Blake came to visit he could draw his own conclusions. After all, we hadn't seen the place ourselves and couldn't describe it to him.

Finally, it was time to call. My stomach tightened, and I felt myself perspire in the air-conditioned room. I started to dial, got mixed up in the middle, and slowly redialed. Our friend answered.

"Hey, Betty,* it's Steve. How's everything going?"

"Not very well, really—wait a minute. I'd like Bill* to speak with you."

When Bill picked up the phone, he didn't pause to greet me. "Blake is distraught. He's right here and needs to talk with you."

"Okay," I said fearfully, "put him on."

"Daddy, why are you going to jail?"

He will never know how those sobbed-out words cut into my heart. He could only assume that I had lied to him. I wondered how a five-year-old could bear the pain he was feeling. I wanted to reach through the telephone wire and hold him. Unprepared for his question, I nearly dropped the phone and started to cry myself.

"No, Blake. I'm calling from Florida at a place where Mommy, Liz, and I are staying." Even though my voice sounded under control, my body shook. Anger flooded through me. We had told our friends how we chose to handle the situation. Apparently they had shown no respect for our judgment. Who had mentioned "jail" to Blake?

"Daddy, Janie told me you're going to prison. Are you going to *jail*?"

"Son, it's like I told you this morning. Daddy did some things wrong in business, and I'm going to a place in Florida for punishment. It's not a jail—not a real jail—but some people might call it that. It's a work camp for daddies who have made mistakes."

"Then you *are* going to prison, aren't you? What did you do?" The sound of betrayal careened through the line.

"Honey, please don't cry." I couldn't restrain my own tears any longer, and I handed the phone to Harvey. What more could I possibly say? How could he absorb even the best explanation? No judge in the world could have imposed a tougher sentence on me than the one that had just transpired.

Harvey spoke to Blake for about ten minutes with generous assistance from Liz and ended with, "We'll call you tomorrow. Dad and I love you more than anything in the world, and things aren't nearly as bad as you think. Will you please put Mrs. Ramsey* on the phone again?"

Then to Betty, she said, "If Blake has any more rough times between now and the time we're scheduled to call tomorrow, phone us here right away, no matter the hour."

Betty secured our number, assuring Harvey that they hadn't been the ones to upset Blake. Harvey was courteous but didn't sound as though she believed that. After she had hung up the phone, Harvey and I held each other tightly.

Putting an arm around each of us, Liz prayed softly, asking for God's peace for us, for Blake, and for the Ramsey family.

After that, both Harvey and I relaxed. I had some trouble getting to sleep, but I kept reminding myself that I could do nothing to change the situation. Nevertheless, Blake's face came to me again and again, the one showing his current pain as well as the happy face of the times before this day.

To our relief, we learned the next morning that he'd done fine and was already out swimming. We also learned how Blake had heard the word *jail*. One of the little girls had prayed for me. For a long while, I'd been the object of family prayer in their household. The word had slipped out, something entirely unavoidable, and the child didn't realize at the time that she had done anything wrong.

We had long planned for this particular Saturday. Harvey and I took a long walk on the beach, talking and praying. The touch of her hand on mine was a great reassurance.

Later, we drove out to the prison camp near Fort Walton Beach airport and located on the Eglin Air Force Base to see how it looked.

As we approached the place, conversation in the car died. Even Liz, who was driving, had retreated into silence. Just how bad could bad be? This was the place where the courts said I would spend the better part of eight years.

We could hardly believe what we saw. It was beautiful. Bright green, neatly trimmed lawns surrounded a complex that looked much more like a small college campus than a prison. It had none of the towers, barbed wire, or high walls associated with prison life.

We immediately thought of Blake and were thrilled that he would see me here, in such a nonthreatening atmosphere. We quickly agreed that Harvey and Blake should make the trip in two weeks, giving me time to get acclimated. By the time we drove away from Eglin Federal Prison camp, the atmosphere in the car had changed considerably. The tension was still present, but the future had taken on tangible proportions, which were easier to deal with than imaginations gone wild.

Since it would take seven hours to drive from the church in Destin to Atlanta, with another hour added because of the time difference, we decided that Harvey and Liz would leave me around noon, during the church service, the next day. That way they could pick up Blake by eight o'clock that night.

It was prearranged for me to meet a couple at St. Andrew's By-the-Sea Episcopal Church. Longtime members there, Rick and Dottie had an incredible ministry of hospitality. They had offered to bring me home from church with them and later drop me off at Eglin Federal Prison Camp. Although we had never met before, they had agreed to open their home and their lives to me, a complete stranger, after the long-distance introduction from a mutual friend.

Saturday night, as Harvey and I lay in bed together for what we knew would be the last time for a long while, reality hit us. We could only hold one another and keep repeating that we loved each other.

I have since learned that fear indicates a faith in the enemy's ability, but that evening I was fearful. Every worry came to me at once. *How would Harvey and Blake make it financially? Would Blake be okay? Could Harvey handle the loneliness? The rejection? Would our marriage—could our marriage—survive?*

How long would I be away? Would I be safe? I'd heard stories. How real was the chance of being beaten . . . or raped?

In the silent room, as the hour grew later, Harvey had her own thoughts and questions, some too personal, I imagined, even to share with me. That troubled me because I wanted to share every thought, every breath.

Harvey's and my strength since becoming Christians was privately talking with God, praying in quietness. Yet we both realized our need for both God and human contact. We were able to air our distraught feelings and receive comfort from God and from each other. Finally, my hand on hers, I drifted off to sleep. I didn't wake up until morning.

St. Andrew's By-the-Sea afforded Harvey, Liz, and me the sort of worship each of us needed. St. Andrew's has a memorable choir, one of the most beautiful I'd ever heard. As the service progressed, Harvey and I held hands, not daring to look at one another for fear of crying.

Before the service concluded, the three of us slipped out of church, walking slowly toward the car in an attempt to stall our good-byes. Liz walked several paces ahead, allowing us what privacy she could.

It was so impossible! *How in the world am I going to say good-bye to Harvey?* Surely this wasn't happening! It was a bad dream, and Harvey would shake me awake and say, "Stephen, are you all right? You were crying out in your sleep."

I reached inside the car and picked up a large paper sack that held the few things we assumed they'd allow me to take into the prison. I quickly kissed Harvey good-bye, thanked Liz for all her help, and then assisted them into the car. I kept taking deep breaths. It had hurt and been rough, but we had handled it well.

I turned, walked away, and was within a few steps of the church door when I saw the car begin to pull away. Suddenly the tears came. Springs of water erupted from the places my eyes were meant to occupy.

The car passed, and I saw the face of a person I had loved with all my heart from almost the first moment I met her. Now she was being carried away from a husband who had promised to love and provide for her.

I stopped, unable to enter the church because of my uncontrolled sobbing. A few years earlier I'd had every material thing a person could ask from life—expensive cars, a beautiful home, closets filled with good clothes, wonderful vacations. Now, I stood in an unfamiliar parking lot clutching a paper bag filled with just a few possessions that remained from my old life: a pair of tennis shoes, sweat socks, my Bible, and shaving gear.

I felt completely empty, without hope. The enormous pain of the past and the tragedy of the present hit me as never before. At that moment there seemed to be nothing to hope for. I had no future.

Then the car stopped and backed up. Harvey ran to me in an instant, and I buried my face in the crook of her neck.

"Please don't cry, honey," she said. It sounded like she was begging. "Everything will be okay. I love you so much."

I nodded, my face still pressed against her, unable to speak.

"If you make it back into church, I know you'll feel better," she said.

I nodded, and we kissed. We didn't allow our eyes to meet. She got into the car, and they began to drive away. My emotions gave way again, and the scene was repeated, her coming to me, speaking words of assurance, her lingering embrace, and the loving good-bye. This time, I managed to regain enough composure to walk back into the church.

Who started the rumor that women are the weaker sex? As I relive that parting scene, I still marvel at Harvey's strength. She was much stronger than I. Strong enough that I could draw strength from her.

Once inside the church, I dropped my paper bag beside the door and crept into a pew near the back. The serving of Holy Communion began. The choir sang softly, and people from the front rows advanced toward the altar to kneel. Because of the size of the congregation, I knew it would be only a few minutes before my turn came.

I thought the worst was over, but the pain returned, and so did the tears. I felt helpless, awkward, foolish, as the sobbing stranger in the back pew. But mostly I missed Harvey and wanted to touch her, to take Communion with her. I wanted my best friend. When the usher stood at my pew I could hardly make the effort, but the whole row of people waited for me.

My handkerchief never left my face. I knelt to receive the elements that symbolize our Lord's broken body and his blood. The priests offered me the sacraments. A woman knelt beside me. I felt her soft hand on mine, holding it tightly. I returned the grasp. It seemed that God had sent the woman by proxy, for Harvey. Here was the hand I needed, the strength from another person. I was not alone.

Since that time, I have thought of the biblical story of the woman who anointed Jesus's head with costly perfume. It seemed a small act—even a foolish one, to some people— but Jesus had said, "Wherever this gospel is preached throughout the world, what she has done will also be told, in memory of her" (Matthew 26:13). In that same spirit I will always remember Carolyn, the woman who comforted me by her touch.

The two priests, knowing nothing about me and yet sensitive to the crisis of the moment, came over and rested their hands tenderly on my head and prayed. Those prayers, and especially Carolyn's hand, brought me to a place of peace. I didn't need to cry anymore. As I knelt there in that Episcopal church, surrounded by strangers—yet brothers and sisters in the faith—the Lord provided the kind of inner strength I needed. I could even offer a weak smile to those around me.

A few moments later, the worship service ended. Parishioners adjourned to an adjacent building for coffee and fellowship. I went there and sought out the Culps, the man and wife my friend had told me about. Since both of them sang in the choir, we had arranged to meet after the service. Warm and open people, they immediately welcomed me.

After a short while, I felt amazingly well—and loved. Sorrow and guilt were in the distance; my concern centered around Harvey. She had a long drive from Destin to Atlanta, and she was returning to some heavy responsibilities. I was relieved she was with Liz rather than making the trip alone.

I knew that for me this period of peace and composure was God's grace and sent up a silent prayer of thanks, knowing he would afford Harvey the same gift.

Harvey was suffering her own fears. She wrote: "Driving away from the church, my head throbbed with pain. I instinctively rubbed my forehead and temples, trying to rub the hurt away, but no relief could be found. The sunlight hurt my eyes so I closed them, but I knew rest would be impossible.

"Fear translated itself to tightness in my chest and shortness of breath. I directed the air conditioner vent to my face. Liz was considerate enough not to talk and invade my turmoil, so at least I didn't have to process my thoughts for conversation.

"In just forty-eight hours my life had fallen apart. I had watched my little boy say good-bye to the father he adores. Now, on a more adult level, I was saying good-bye to my very best friend. *Could this be happening?* I cried silently. At the same time, I told myself that I must be in control and pull myself together. I had so much responsibility; I had to be a good witness. But that was stupid! I wasn't capable of anything—outside of God's intervening. I prayed desperately just to be able to make it through. I begged for God's help. Without realizing it, I turned Stephen over to God's care at that moment. I couldn't begin to carry his pain as well as my own."

After brunch the Culps took me home with them. Rick and I spent the afternoon walking and chatting on the beach. After dinner, we drove to hear the St. Andrew's By-the-Sea choir sing at a neighboring church. And then they drove me to Eglin, my work camp—and home—for the years ahead.

In the car I asked, "Rick, would you do me a favor and call Harvey when you get home? She should be in Atlanta in another hour. When she drove away I was a mess. Would you tell her that I'm all right? *Really* all right!"

"Of course." He smiled and patted my shoulder. "'I had planned to call anyway."

I thanked him for that kindness. "And tell her that although the day started as the worst day of my life, after Communion and my afternoon with you and Dottie, it became one of the nicest, most tranquil days in my memory."

"That's wonderful," Rick said. "Do you want us to tell her anything else?"

"Just tell her that somehow I feel ready to go now. I feel prepared for whatever the future holds."

The headlights brought my new home-away-from-home into view. In another moment we parked. Rick, Dottie, and I shared a brief prayer. Then I headed inside. As I waved good-bye, I was at peace.

*Chapter 3*

*Chapter 3*

# ON THE INSIDE

"Okay, Lawson, pick up that pile of clothes over there and follow me," barked the guard.

"Yes, sir," I answered. "Do you want me to change now?"

"Lawson, when I want you to change clothes I'll tell you to change clothes. I said 'follow me.' Are you going to follow me or stand there and ask a lot of stupid questions? You might have been a big shot on the outside, but that crap doesn't fly here. Understand?"

"Yes, sir."

I followed him to a small room that contained shelves of blankets and sheets on one wall and hanging rods of civilian clothes on the other two.

"Okay, Lawson," said the guard as he sat down on the only chair in the room. "Strip down, and stand in front of me when you've finished."

I undressed and stood three feet in front of him. The guard, making no effort to disguise his personal disdain toward all prisoners and perhaps the tough breaks he had endured to have to take a job like this, stood up, toe-to-toe with me. As he gave his next command I would feel the warmth and smell the foul odor of his nicotine breath.

"Put your hands over your head."

Without comment, I complied. His hands ran over my body and through my hair. He made it a point to look closely at all major veins to determine if I mainlined drugs.

I had played basketball all through school and even as an adult had been in many locker rooms and never considered myself particularly modest. But this process went beyond a matter of modesty; it was dehumanizing. He didn't miss an inch of my body. "Bend over!" He picked up a flashlight and inspected my rectum. I found out later that all prisoners are treated that way, in order to prevent them from smuggling in drugs.

The strongest possible statement about my role as a prisoner had been made by this initiation. Within minutes I knew I had left my old life in the past. I had lost ordinary rights. I learned quickly that I was in prison and under the total authority of others. For whatever time I was there I would be subject to the authority of guards who had a life sentence of their own and had become horribly jaded in the process. Prisoners would serve their time and go home. The guards, however, stayed on with no time off for good behavior. Almost every contact with them indicated the same thought process: we were there to be punished as opposed to being there as punishment.

Then we finished the rest of the process—mug shots and personal information. It was assembly-line automatic. Another guard assigned me a cot, then sheets, blankets, and pillowcases. I dressed in my prison clothing issue of steel-toe shoes, secondhand blue Air Force shirts and pants, T-shirts, socks, and underwear.

Since it was eleven at night, long past lights out, I had to make my bed in the dark, stuffing my other new possessions in a foot locker alongside. I guessed about thirty people slept in the barracks. Large fans stirred the stale, humid air. The loud droning of the fans combined with snoring noises from around the room provided an alien, disconcerting backdrop for my first night's sleep.

I lay on my back, thinking. Harvey, Blake, and I recently had begun a fabulous walk with God. I even felt a strange sort of prospective excitement about the sort of credibility our witness would bring, secure in the knowledge of knowing it wasn't where you served that mattered—but who you served.

I knew I belonged to the Lord. Jesus Christ had taken me into protective custody. Rather than "doing time," time would become my ally. I silently pledged myself to learning God's Word so that one day, when I left, I would be a lot stronger than when I arrived. I also had the assurance that, even though Harvey and I were apart, prison could not truly separate us any more than it could separate me from the love of Jesus Christ.

With this assurance, I prayed for my family and slipped into a solid sleep, broken only hours later by a gruff voice over a loud speaker that heralded in my first day "on the inside."

As the others got out of bed I noticed they left their beds unmade. Not knowing what to do or where to go, I decided to copy the movements of others. I quickly dressed in the clothes I had taken off the night before and grabbed for my toilet articles. I followed the traffic pattern to a large bathroom that contained two dozen sinks, with as many urinals and shower stalls.

A wave of nausea hit me as I stared at the room. The floors were filthy, the garbage containers were overflowing, and most sinks were covered with bits of hair and soap-scum rings. The subdued atmosphere prevailed with hardly a word passing between the men. Each person was trying to focus his eyes and get started for the day.

I shaved and washed my face and hands quickly and, still following the traffic pattern, made my way back to my cot. No one had yet made his bed, and I vaguely wondered why because I felt reasonably sure that no one else would come in to do it. The traffic moved ahead and out of the building. I followed.

I was totally alone. I knew no one. Steve Lawson, the super-salesman, the man always at ease with people, now didn't know how to get acquainted and break the ice. That had never stopped me before when I went into a room filled with strangers. But it was different now. Everything was different. Worst of all, I didn't know any of the rules.

I was half afraid to make any associations. Suppose the person I spent time with was disliked by others and it made me guilty by association? *Would I be safe here?* Several inmates gave me the impression they could get quite physical if the situation called for it. Over the past few months I had heard many pitiful tales of violence and rape. *What would it be like in the showers?* I saw an immediate dilemma. I didn't want to shower with a crowd of others, but on the other hand, I didn't want to be caught alone in there either.

As I followed the flow of men, all my worst fears came back. Every terrible worry hit as if for the first time. How would I survive here for the better part of eight years? How could Harvey and Blake make it on the outside? Would I even have a family once all this was over? Would it ever really be over? My heart crashed inside me like a sledgehammer.

We came into the mess hall, and for the first time, the men talked among themselves. I ate in silence and listened to the general comments of other prisoners. Many found fault with everything and everyone. No one said a word to me. And for the first time in my life, I said nothing to a single person—there in that mess hall filled with about 350 men, seated at tables for four. I was surprised to find that the breakfast included a good menu that featured pancakes.

Some of the inmates seemed to be in good spirits, and the guards acted friendly enough, although aloof.

Then it was back to the barracks for bed-making, orientation lectures, a tour of the compound followed by a literacy test, physical exam, and job assignment.

My first two weeks at Eglin revolved around barracks duty of cleaning urinals, vacuuming floors, cleaning windows, and emptying garbage cans. The free enterprise system does not exist in prison, and every inmate moves at a snail's pace. I tried to do my work cheerfully. I don't know how well I succeeded, but I kept asking God to give me strength and not to let me feel sorry for myself. I also knew that it had to get better.

But on that first day, I realized something that would help me "do time" much more easily. It's a simple concept, but it made the difference for me: *nothing about the system ever seems reasonable.* At that moment, I determined not to let illogical and unfair things bother me. I now lived in an illogical and unreasonable world. I asked God for a generous sense of humor so I could see the comical side of things. In time, that decision would prove invaluable.

*Chapter 4*

# CELEBRATIONS

P rison allows plenty of time for introspection, and I thought a great deal about my earlier life and all that had gone on before. Naturally, I reflected on all the mistakes I had made. Also, I thought a lot about my family, about growing up, and particularly about the reasons involved with the decisions I had made.

First of all, I believe that each person is responsible for his or her own choices. I went to prison for acts I committed, knowing full well that I had been wrong. I would never lay my guilt at the feet of my parents or anyone else. But it can be a healing and helpful process to understand the difficulties and hurts of life and to see how those things impacted your life. It's been said that a person lives at home for his first eighteen years and then spends the rest of his life attempting to deal with those years. A few significant events in my background helped shape me into the Stephen Lawson who married Harvey, fathered Blake, and had a lot of business success, then lost it all and went to prison.

I was born to Sanford and Lillian Lawson in 1937. It was the second marriage for each and in retrospect appeared happy as long as my father remained successful. For my first ten years, I remember Dad as a successful dress manufacturer with office and showrooms in New York City and mills in Worcester, Massachusetts. We lived on a beautiful estate in Kings Point, near Long Island Sound.

Our family included Rosemary, my sister from Mother's first marriage. Rosemary is twelve years older than I am, and I didn't know she was my half-sister until I was thirteen. I just thought of her as the faultless sister, the one I was expected to emulate in personality, manners, and schoolwork. Rosemary and I laugh at that today because she recalls a lot of parental discipline for someone considered so perfect.

Since I was in grade school when Rosemary married Arthur and moved away, we didn't grow up very close. Our parents, until the year Rosemary married, enjoyed a great deal of prosperity. They entertained lavishly and kept our stately home crowded with guests.

Rosemary remembers Dad as the dominant parent. Her memories recall him as demanding, even authoritarian, and not particularly understanding or considerate. She points out that he was short, uneducated, and came from England without a dime in his pocket yet had made it big. He wore his success like an upper-class Englishman wears his school tie. He ordered Mother around as if she were an underling created to carry out his commands.

Since Dad had lost all his money by the time I turned thirteen, my life—and perceptions of my parents—differed considerably from Rosemary's. After Dad's business losses, he developed heart problems and then strokes. His financial failures also took their toll. The Dad I knew was a lamb compared to the lion of Rosemary's memory. I'd always considered him the victim, whereas she had seen him as the villain.

I pictured Mother as the dominant person in our household. She was a tiger! A wounded tiger, doubtless, with an accumulation of hurts and scars that caused her to attack the ones she loved—especially her husband and her son.

However, during my early years on our estate, life was uncomplicated and most enjoyable. I went to summer camp in New Hampshire, had long romps with my collie on our spacious lawn, and played with many friends. Despite the dreamlike quality of those times, I felt that something was wrong—something I couldn't consciously identify.

My seventh birthday party brought these feelings sharply into focus. Dad and Mother went to enormous trouble and expense. There were Uncle Remus characters molded from ice cream, multicolored balloons, and a magician's act. The extensive guest list included children of my parents' friends plus a few of my schoolmates.

I had already begun to realize the importance of impressions. My parents taught by example. They always associated with the right people and encouraged me to be friendly with their children. The public school I attended also had children from less-privileged circumstances. I should have been thrilled about the party my parents had planned for me. But even at age seven I knew that the party was as much for their benefit as mine.

I still have vivid memories of my guests arriving. Kids my age, well-polished and dressed in their best party clothes, each arrived with a beautifully wrapped present and handed it to me as my folks and I greeted them at the door. Of all the guests, I wanted to see Jane Bullock* most of all. To me, she was the most beautiful girl who had ever lived, and I imagined that we would grow up and get married someday. I explained my feelings to my parents as we stood by the door, and I begged them not to ask what her father did or where they lived. Jane's father had died, and she and her mother lived in a modest apartment behind the post office in nearby Great Neck. I knew there was a difference between their situation and ours, and I didn't want her to feel out of place.

Someone in an old car let Jane off at the base of our driveway. She was not dressed as richly as the other children. But she still looked great to me. She didn't have a boxed gift but handed me a birthday card. Inside the envelope she had placed a brand new one-dollar bill.

"Hello, honey," Mother said and then commented on how pretty Jane looked and how pleased she was to meet her. Her tone of voice did not make the comments sound believable. I felt awful.

It got worse. "Where do you live, honey?" Mother continued and asked, "What does your father do?" I was totally embarrassed and humiliated for Jane and furious with Mother.

That night I took the dollar bill Jane had given me and wrote "I love Jane Bullock, May 24, 1944" across the face.

Seventeen years later, on a Saturday night, I happened to be back in that old neighborhood on business. At day's end, I took some time to reminisce as I drove by old landmarks. I was amazed to find my favorite delicatessen still in business and stopped in for a corned beef sandwich.

As I savored the mingled scents of kosher pickles, salamis, and myriad other meats and spices in that place, I noticed a couple about my age who sat several tables over. The woman was facing me, and I was jolted with recognition. On impulse, I walked over to them.

"Excuse me," I said. "I don't mean to interrupt. But are you Jane Bullock, by any chance?"

"It used to be," she smiled, "but now it's Westmoreland.*"

"I'm Steve Lawson, and—"

"Oh my gosh! Jason,* this is Steve Lawson. We were in first grade together, and I was crazy about him. I almost died when he moved away." Jason laughed good-naturedly at Jane's animated introduction and invited me to join them.

I sat down, and Jane and I recalled old times. Before long, she brought up that long-ago birthday party. "It was the most beautiful party I have ever been to in my entire life."

I stared in disbelief. All those years, I'd carried the hurt of that moment when she had walked through our door and was met by Mother's inquisition. Yet Jane's memory was completely different. It was a moment she had never remembered and one I had never forgotten. Then I noticed she was wearing a corsage. She explained that it was her birthday.

"If I'd known we would meet tonight," I said, "I would have bought a present for you, with the hope that you would love it as much as I loved the present you gave me. Do you remember that present?"

"You're embarrassing me, Steve. I have no idea."

I reached inside my sport jacket for my pocket secretary, fished in one of its compartments, and pulled out the dollar bill. I handed it to Jane.

She opened the folded bill and stared down at what was undeniably the handwriting of a seven-year-old. "I love Jane Bullock. May 24, 1944." When she looked up again there were tears in her eyes.

When I turned twelve, we moved to Worcester. That move ended an era. We lived there less than two years, yet I recall that period with sadness because, by then, Dad knew he would soon be out of business and broke. During that period, unnoticed at the top of the stairway in our rented house on Beechmont Road, I often listened to my parents' conversations about divorce.

At times Mother vented her frustration at him through furious tirades about me, making terrible and untrue accusations concerning my conduct and lack of honesty. Many times she would corner me and shout, "You're just like your father! You're going to end up just like him!" I resented her slandering my father, and I hated her accusations against me. Although falsely accused, I was helpless to rebut her. It became clear that Dad had a wife he didn't care for and that I had a mother I didn't much like either. The yelling became a pattern of life.

I desired to celebrate my bar mitzvah in Worcester on my thirteenth birthday. My folks, not being particularly religious, had never expressed any interest in my fulfilling that Jewish ritual, but it was something I wanted to do badly. Accordingly, they arranged for me to take Hebrew lessons six months before the big date. Three days a week I walked over to Rabbi Bernstein's* house after school.

The rabbi lived in a modest neighborhood in an unpretentious white house with a wraparound porch. Inside, Rabbi and Mrs. Bernstein kept the boxy rooms dimly lit, with lace doilies of various shapes and sizes carefully placed on every available flat surface.

Mrs. Bernstein was a stout woman with a sweet, if somewhat formal, spirit. She spoke with the trace of a European accent and wore her hair pulled taut into a bun on the back of her head. I remember Rabbi Bernstein as thin, clean shaven, and wearing black horn-rimmed spectacles. He always dressed in a black suit with an undistinguished necktie.

As Mrs. Bernstein entered the room bearing a snack for a hungry boy who was already apprehensive about the task he couldn't possibly complete, Rabbi Bernstein was impatient to start.

"Sarah, the boy isn't here to have dinner. He's here to learn Hebrew in six months, which he should have been devoting himself to over the past six years."

He then lapsed into Yiddish for Mrs. Bernstein. In a few moments she was gone, shaking her head, never to return. Now it was Rabbi Bernstein and Master Lawson, one-on-one.

He didn't say it, but the attitude was more than clear. How could I have the *chutzpah*—the gall—to show up at this rabbi's house and expect to be ready for a bar mitzvah in six months when it takes everyone else in the world year after year of study?

I had no doubt in my mind that I could do it. It wasn't long, however, before a gathering fog of futility descended upon Rabbi Bernstein. A few months passed with no visible sign of improvement. Even I had become disenchanted with the whole idea. Another month passed. Rabbi Bernstein grew concerned, and I became disillusioned. Soon the rabbi was in a state of panic.

One Wednesday I walked into his study, and Rabbi Bernstein looked up with a trace of a smile on his lips—a treat he seldom afforded himself. With a burst of ingenuity, he shared a plan intended to save both our reputations, especially his.

"Stephen, there is only a little over two months left before your bar mitzvah. It should be apparent that if we continue as we have been going, there is no possibility that you can be prepared. I don't know what you've been doing in temple all those years prior to moving here, but learning Hebrew wasn't included."

I laughed in embarrassment.

"Therefore, I have written your entire bar mitzvah phonetically underneath the Hebrew, to aid you in your studies."

Obviously, he was imploring me to stop studying and start memorizing.

After that, my studies progressed at a splendid rate. Soon I'd memorized the entire Hebrew portion with minimum mispronunciation. And it seemed that Rabbi Bernstein was pleased with the patriarchal prerogative he had initiated.

For me, neither the pile of customary presents nor the idea of being the leading man in a "play" had spurred me on. It was simple, really; an entire family would respond to the bar mitzvah event. Aunts and uncles would come from out of town, and there'd be a festive mood. If I did well, they'd all congratulate my parents, who couldn't help but be proud of me. I wanted their love more than anything else in the world.

I had somehow come to believe that the constant fighting at home must be my fault. All my attempts at improving my daily behavior seemed to have failed. I was surrounded by vigilant suspicion and dislike. I needed this bar mitzvah. It was the big event, the success required to undo all the harm I thought I had caused.

On that day, my folks drove me to the temple. Their serene behavior let me know that they were pleased to be a part of my big day. When I walked out to the pulpit with the rabbi and sat in a chair beside his, they smiled at me.

The cantor sat on the other side of the ark, which contained the Holy Scrolls, the Torah. As I looked out into the congregation, I could see almost every seat was taken. My bar mitzvah was made a part of a regular worship service, which accounted for the large attendance. In the first row, where members of my family sat, I saw huge smiles, waving hands, and other signals of encouragement.

Finally, my moment arrived. As I rose to accompany the rabbi to the ark to bring the Torah to the pulpit, my heart rejoiced. All the months of work had been worth it. Nothing could distract me. My parents showed their obvious pleasure. The day was turning out to be all I could have wished for.

The ark door opened, revealing the Torah, the embodiment of the Jewish faith. It contains the terms of the Jews' covenant with God. As the rabbi lifted the Torah from the ark and placed it in my arms, I looked at him. Rabbi Bernstein's entire existence was wrapped around and interwoven with the Torah and its teachings.

Suddenly, I felt like a fraud. Worse, I knew I was a fraud. I wanted to run. Oh, God, what had I done? If there really was a God, could he forgive me for what I had done and the mess I was in the midst of?

As we approached the pulpit, my family's encouraging expressions suddenly filled me with dismay. Though my parents knew I'd memorized rather than learned the Hebrew, they didn't seem to share the utter shame that I felt. My own despair contrasted oddly with the carnival atmosphere in the first row, the hand gestures that indicated "Go get 'em, tiger!" and "Do us proud, son."

Relatives nudged each other with expectation. They were primed to share in my moment—a moment I recognized as a bizarre piece of play-acting.

The Torah was placed on the pulpit and opened. So much Hebrew, and I didn't know one letter from the next. Standing at my side with great bearing, the rabbi picked up a long silver pointer and placed it beside a symbol on the right-hand side of a line halfway down the scroll. He nodded his head for me to begin, much as a symphony conductor might communicate with his orchestra. I had no idea what I must do.

"*Baruch et* Adonai," the rabbi suggested in a whisper. His lips never moved. I glanced at him. "*Baruch et* Adonai," came the plea once more. Again, his lips did not move.

"*Baruch et* Adonai," I began. "*Baruch* Adonai *ham'vorach l'olam va'ed*." Wonder of wonders, Rabbi Bernstein's pointer on the Torah was moving with the words I was muttering.

I stopped thinking about fraud and concentrated on the business I had prepared for.

Words tumbled out of my mouth as the pointer moved faster. My fans in the front row were ecstatic. Now it wasn't enough to merely recite what I'd learned, so I began to ham it up, putting great emphasis on various words so as to produce a dramatic reading. The silver pointer could hardly keep up, and the rabbi gave a few quick glances in my direction. He must have thought I'd gone mad.

At last the ceremony ended. I accepted the congratulations of my parents and other relatives while the rabbi stood silently watching. I couldn't turn around and meet his eyes, because I felt so guilty for what I had done.

I had been a fraud. But on the other hand, what did it really matter? I had pleased my folks. Rabbi Bernstein, after all, had conceived and condoned the plan. Obviously, the end had justified the means.

That day a bad lesson in ethics got stored away for future use. In the years that followed, I learned to rationalize just about anything on the basis of doing what I considered the situation demanded. Worst of all, I gave no thought to where such situational ethics or actions would eventually lead.

# Chapter 5

# LEARNING TO GAMBLE

Dad went out of business a year later, and we moved to St. Louis. I enjoyed it there, though my school work started to decline. Life at home was hard, and never a day passed without turmoil. It didn't let up even when Dad became sick. He suffered a major stroke which left him unable to speak. He had to take speech lessons, and though years later I could discern no problems, Dad always felt his speech to be a second or two slower than his thought processes.

During the time Dad couldn't talk, it seemed that Mother yelled at him even louder. My heart would break as tears rolled down Dad's face, and I heard his sobs. At such times I realized, quite consciously, that I hated my mother. I loved her too, strangely, but would have run away except that I couldn't desert Dad. Every time she exploded in bitterness, her anger infected everyone around her.

Soon it seemed best for me to live with an aunt in Louisville while Dad and Mother moved to Milwaukee, where he could be under the care of a specialist. I was relieved to escape our home situation yet also tremendously sad. Dad was so sick that I wondered if I'd be saying good-bye to him for the last time.

I will forever remember the day they left for Milwaukee. I crossed the wet lawn after checking our empty apartment; Mother wanted to make sure they'd left nothing behind. It was a difficult moment, and I knew that saying good-bye to Dad would be emotional.

Suddenly, Mother sprang from the car and headed toward me with spiteful determination. She shouted about my ruining my shoes on the wet lawn and claimed I didn't show concern about anything. As usual, she tried to slap me. And, as usual, she used a right-hand lead, so I blocked it with little effort.

Because of that episode, one of my life's touching moments had been aborted. The good-bye was quick. I felt no compassion or love for either of them as they drove away.

In Louisville, I experienced the happiest days of my adolescence. At age fifteen, I found myself to be extremely popular and was continually in the middle of exciting happenings. After eighteen months there, I rejoined my parents in New York City.

Nothing had changed. I could feel the tension and un-happiness a mile away. We lived at the Bolivar, a residential hotel located on Central Park West at Eighty-Third Street. We had one bedroom, one bath, and a tiny Pullman-type kitchen. I slept on a convertible sofa in the living room, and Mother cooked meals on a hot plate and a portable rotisserie grill.

Dad's health seemed greatly improved, but it gradually failed over the next ten years until his death. He held several jobs during that time but was often unemployed. He became a textile salesman, working on straight commissions for people he otherwise wouldn't have associated with. He had to carry his heavy samples from account to account. He wasn't given good accounts to service and continually struggled to establish new ones for himself. Physically, he couldn't handle it; he'd come home each night exhausted. During those times I learned how much I respected this man and, yes, how much I loved him. Until his death, he stayed optimistic about his future and held on to the sincere belief that things would be better. He never stopped trying.

To Mother's credit, she encouraged him to use the portable sunlamp each night so he'd present a prosperous, healthy appearance. Also, she'd iron his dress shirts and make sure they were perfectly wrinkle free, even if she did complain loudly as she did them. Those memories still linger, and even now, I much prefer to send everything out to be laundered—and not to see my wife, Harvey, standing behind an ironing board.

For years, Dad had made every effort to pay his creditors back. He had borrowed large sums of money to keep his former business afloat and couldn't imagine not honoring his debts. But finally he did go bankrupt. It seemed at that time that he had reached a poverty of soul as well. Lists were made of everything we could possibly need in the foreseeable future, everything from socks and underwear to bedding, furniture, radios, television sets, and expensive clothing. "If we're going to have the stigma of being bankrupt, we might as well go about it in the right way. If you're going to have the name, you might as well play the game," Mom would say, enjoying this time of sudden affluence. Every credit card they owned and department store charge account they had were used, abused, and added to the list of creditors at the time Dad filed for bankruptcy.

Mother would take me shopping. "My son would like to see a suit in a banker's gray. Is this the best material you have? I don't like the feel of it at all!" she'd storm. "Yes, that's much better. I understand it's in quite another price range than the other suit, but 'cheap *is* cheap.' When you know quality you can't settle for less," Mom would go on in expansive bellows of self-congratulation. In all honesty, I enjoyed the new clothes every bit as much as the jokes Mother and I would secretly share in front of the salesperson that was writing up the order and charging it to our account. "Steve, I'm glad you listened to your mother," she would say. "It's more money, but when it comes to dressing my son right, money is no object." I was a willing student in another lesson in situational ethics.

Other parts of our existence weren't nearly as pleasant. My mother and father went through ritualistic periods of guilt, concern, and remorse. They felt martyred by the neglect of friends who had faded away. Dad no longer wore a flower in his lapel. In the past, when we'd known prosperity, his money seemed to give him a certain aura. Now he looked and acted like any other short, uneducated, and unhappy man.

Dad attempted suicide when I was twenty-three by taking an overdose of sleeping pills and was saved through my administering mouth-to-mouth resuscitation until the paramedics came. He was rushed to the hospital, where after a touch-and-go thirty-six hours, he pulled through. I found the bitter note he left for Mother and made sure she never saw it. In it, Dad claimed he'd taken the only way he knew to escape her. The overdose was her fault as much as if she had pulled the trigger of a gun, he wrote. As life continued with little tranquility or peace, I often felt I had done Dad a disservice by reviving him that evening.

It was during the period at the end of high school and the beginning of college that two major beginnings took place in my life: gambling and the horrible feelings of loneliness that would recur at significant points in my life.

To assuage those episodes of shattering desolation, I often attended services at the temple. But religion didn't satisfy the emptiness. I even attempted to read the Bible—the Old Testament, of course, since I didn't know anyone who owned a New Testament. Somehow I sensed a spiritual void. I started at the beginning and read most of Genesis before putting the book down as too unbelievable. I continued life on my own—and alone.

By this time I was a student at New York University. My life suffered even more in comparison to that of some of my friends. Peter continually bought expensive clothes; Ronnie purchased a new car; David spent summers at the Lido Beach Club; and Norm was able to save his money and use it however he wished. Not so for me. I perceived that I was part of a caste system in which things could not possibly improve.

Everyone I knew had much the same things in common. They ate Chinese food on Sundays, played gin rummy at the club, and loved to bet on a ball game. Not only that, everyone, but everyone, had a bookmaker.

If you didn't have your own bookmaker but attended a game at Madison Square Garden, it didn't matter since there were more bookmakers in The Garden than paying fans, it seemed. The truth is, most of my friends enjoyed the status of having a personal bookmaker. With this dubious honor came the recognition that someone believed in you enough to provide a line of credit that no bank, certainly, would extend.

Since I wasn't able to bet enough to have my own account, for many years, I bet through others. That posed no restriction, since people welcomed additional action on their accounts. Thus they appeared to be bigger bettors than they actually were—a good impression to give a bookmaker. We all learned how to make good impressions—that is to say, puffed-up ones. This became a way of life.

I was in high school when I placed my very first bet. I gambled ten dollars on the N.I.T. basketball finals and watched the game with my heart in my mouth, knowing full well I'd have a hard time coming up with ten dollars if I lost.

Fortunately (or so I thought back then), I won that first bet. When I received my ten-dollar winnings the next week, I experienced the rush of "making it big." I could anticipate more of this easy money since it seemed effortless to pick more winners than losers. Now I could do as much as the next guy and be as big a sport as my friends. Betting offered me a way out of my circumstances. The bet itself was a thrill since it brought excitement into an otherwise dull existence. You see, all the money I made at various jobs went to my parents except for a few dollars I kept for carfare and meals.

I could never buy anything tangible with my winnings, of course, since my folks would be sure to question the source of my money. But I could spend the money on myself and believe I was more like other people—a person of means.

My friend David gave me some helpful tips on conducting myself as a bettor. "The first thing you did wrong when you won that ten dollars was to stop betting. You let the bookie off the hook."

"What do you mean?" I queried. "I won ten dollars, and he paid me."

"That's what I mean. You have no betting mentality. When you were ahead ten dollars, you should have made two other ten-dollar bets. You know that your chances of winning both are much greater than your losing both—aren't they?"

I thought a minute. "Of course."

"Okay then. If you win both, you're up thirty dollars and can sock him a bet—maybe twenty dollars or so. If you split your bet, nothing has been lost, and if you lose both, it's no big deal. After all, you were up ten dollars already, so you'd be only a ten-dollar winning bet away from being even again."

I could see that David was correct. He had also pointed out to me that I had a loser's mentality, a guy who would be grateful for crumbs instead of the sort who'd seize opportunity by the throat and take full advantage.

I concluded that it was the difference between two types of people: those who hadn't experienced all the negatives of life and therefore could still afford to go about living in a rational, meaningful way—and then there was me.

The next several weeks produced the sort of success I could have only dreamed of. I won seventy dollars, ninety-five dollars, ninety dollars. And since I couldn't buy anything tangible, I was able to date. When David and I double-dated, taking the girls out to dinner, I appeared a man of means, as did my friends. I tasted the good life and couldn't imagine ever having a losing week. The fact is, I did lose—and often. Later, I started diverting my paycheck from my folks, offering various excuses. Our relationship grew worse.

I often lied to them, saying that I was to have dinner at a friend's house when, in fact, I was taking a date to one of New York's finest restaurants. Other times, I was at Yonkers Raceway when I had told them I was somewhere else. For the most part, my lies were accepted without question. When they did question what I said, I stayed one step ahead of them, arranging alibis and supporting lies from my friends.

My new life concept had taken firm root. Everything my parents had taught me, everything my friends were showing me, proved the importance of having spendable money in order to make the right impressions. I would look for the best risk-reward ratio. I learned more about the fine points of situational ethics and the best ways to manipulate others through rationalization of conduct.

Like any other person subject to an addiction, I was the last to know or even suspect what was happening. I just knew that betting offered me a chance to enjoy life, and I was confident that I could win much more than I'd lose. It became easy to rationalize any losses as merely bad luck.

My betting started when I was in high school and continued uninterrupted until I was forty-one. That self-deceived mental posture permeated every area of my life and led to my downfall.

Eventually, betting cost me almost everything I had. Some of my bets were bigger than I would ever care to admit. Like many other men addicted to gambling, I grew reckless—with my name, my business, my personal integrity, and eventually even with my wife and child.

*Chapter 6*

# FALLING IN LOVE

Harvey was the first girl I ever dated who was neither Jewish nor wealthy. For twenty-seven years, I figured if I limited my dating to those who were Jewish and had money, I would decrease my chances of marrying some poor gentile. About an hour before we met, I learned that Harvey was Episcopalian.

"That's one rung under Roman Catholic, isn't it?" I asked my friend David.

"I have no idea," he replied, "but they shake hands when they're introduced to you. Can you imagine that? I mean, can you picture a Jewish girl saying, 'It's very nice to meet you' and shaking hands?"

We considered that quite humorous. We dressed British and thought Yiddish, and since we were ignorant, we didn't consider ourselves bigoted.

It was mid-season for the major sports teams. We lived in the East, so we could calculate our winnings from game to game before betting on events about to start on the West Coast. It had been a normal Sunday afternoon, with David and me monitoring our various bets and ball games. The bookmaker's office would be open until eight. Our tab was carried from Tuesday to the following Monday, and by Sunday, we were betting on a per-game basis. We verified that we were ahead but if we were losing, we used Sunday to break even. If ahead, we rationalized that we were betting with their money, so by "laying it in," we could chance to make a lot of money without risk.

By seven that evening we had placed our last bets. David turned off the television set. Peter, an old friend since childhood days, stood idly by. He'd come to watch the games with us but seldom placed a bet. David and I dished out quite a bit of ridicule to Peter, whose conservative attitude toward betting afforded us little in common.

We'd had a good week, and David felt pleased. "Time for Chinese food," he announced briskly. "As a matter of fact, rather than go alone, let's call up a few beautiful girls and ask them to join us."

"Terrific idea, David. Let's do it," I agreed, smiling broadly.

Peter fell right into our ploy. "Hey! All right! Who do you guys have in mind?"

David looked as though Peter were crazy. "Come on, Peter, you're the ladies' man. You always talk about the fabulous girls you meet in the advertising business. If you're not full of baloney, make a phone call. You have enough names to share!"

Peter knew he was trapped. We never supposed that he was the ladies' man he professed to be, but he had been bragging, and it was time to produce. Actually, we didn't think he would come through.

"There are two girls—roommates—who live near here," he said. "I dated the one from Atlanta who moved up here to get into show business. I selected her to be our national Miss Positan, the feminine version of the tanning product, Man-Tan."

"I remember that product. It was taken off the market. She isn't still yellow, is she, Peter? We wouldn't want to be embarrassed by being seen with her on the street," David teased.

"Aw, come on, guys," he responded. "These two shiksa are beautiful and real society types. Are you interested or not?"

"Sure we're interested. Give them a call," I replied.

When Peter got off the phone with some half-baked excuse about striking out, David and I refused to take it lying down. Since they lived close by we'd go to their apartment, uninvited, and see for ourselves what Peter referred to as being beautiful and from real society.

The doorman stopped us, asked us who we were and who we wanted to see. New Yorkers are raised on such challenges as that, so it presented little trouble for us. "Miss Reinhard and Miss Doherty are expecting us. That's the ninth floor, isn't it? Thank you!"

We slipped past him in a flash and into the elevator and within moments were inside with the girls, who were kindly but firmly admonishing Peter for arriving uninvited. We sided with the girls, in a chorus of criticism, telling them they were absolutely correct and that Peter had insisted on bringing us to meet them. Peter wasn't considerate of them at all, we said with feigned annoyance.

Soon Peter, filled with frustration and righteous indignation, made a grandstand move. "Well, if that's the way you feel, I'll leave right now. Come on guys, let's go."

"Peter, why don't you go ahead, and we'll give you a call tomorrow," we chorused.

"The girls are upset, and as long as we interrupted them anyway, we're going to take them out for dinner someplace in the neighborhood so we can say we're sorry." I offered up my most sincere-looking expression. Exit Peter. Enter romance.

Peter wasn't wrong. These girls really were beautiful, especially the blond. At the restaurant our conversation raced along. It was wonderful being with this girl named Harvey.

By dessert, I could contain myself no longer. As Harvey offered me cream for my coffee, I blurted, "No, thanks, but I do take two sugars, and I wish you'd try to remember that because I have a feeling you'll be doing it the rest of your life."

Harvey looked at me incredulously. Her mother had told her that New Yorkers were prone to be crazy, and now she'd met one for sure.

"I beg your pardon," she said. David was right; no Jewish girl would have said, "I beg your pardon."

"Listen, Harvey, I'm not crazy," I began. "I'm twenty-seven and not a guy who falls in love every time he goes out. In fact, I don't think I've dated the same girl twice in a row. But somehow, I know we're going to be married. So as soon as we can get through asking about backgrounds and making small talk we can probably start enjoying a pretty decent relationship."

In years to come, Harvey would relate that she thought I was the craziest person she'd ever met but never the less found me attractive. She says she felt secure with me and that I had the ability to be a good friend. My previous track record of dishonorable intentions with women indicated otherwise, but despite that, Harvey and I became immediate and irrevocable best friends. Her manner advertised her loyalty.

Harvey writes about our first date: "Enter Stephen. He was so nice—almost too nice—and very clean-cut. He had fabulous personality, and was totally engaging. Conversation was very easy. We laughed a lot, and I enjoyed being with him. I had always been attracted to dark, mysterious, and Semitic-looking men. But he was fair-skinned and blue-eyed with light brown—almost blond—hair and had the sweetest face I'd ever seen.

"There we were, on that first date, standing at P.J. Clarke's waiting for a table and holding hands, and I was thinking: *he is the nicest man I have ever met.*"

By the next day, I was telling myself that it wasn't logical to suppose I'd fallen in love with this girl after only three hours the night before. But my thoughts centered on her. Our next date was on her birthday, that Saturday evening. I bought her a simple but beautiful gold pin with rose-colored pearls. It had been a good betting week, and I had the cash; even so, my friends thought I was nuts. "You don't spend fifty dollars on some shiksa you've seen only once!" I invited a few of my friends to dinner so they could meet

Harvey. She was incredibly beautiful and delightful, and she won everyone's heart, especially mine. She still wears the pin.

Although Harvey had specific career goals in mind, her feelings were fast becoming as strong as mine. She would write: "It was disarming, and I was totally unprepared for that turn of events. I had come to New York for a career in theater not for a husband."

Dad took Harvey to his heart immediately. He placed his arm around her and demanded a kiss on his cheek, saying, "We have generations of beautiful women in our family! My father married a beautiful woman, I married a beautiful woman, and it's incumbent on my son also to marry a beautiful woman."

Mother had more of a problem about my dating Harvey than Dad seemed to have. First, Harvey wasn't Jewish. Second, she was in show business. Besides, I couldn't afford to take care of myself, much less a wife. To Mother, who wasn't exactly my biggest fan, the thought of someone having confidence in me and loving me was preposterous. She attempted to negate the relationship using typically non-subtle means.

"Steve, please tell Harvey not to wear false eyelashes so early in the morning. If she must wear them, she should find some that aren't so long."

"Why don't you tell her yourself," I answered curtly, all the while praying for clemency.

Mother started with compliments, telling Harvey she was a beautiful girl, with gorgeous skin and big blue eyes, but that she did have one suggestion, if Harvey didn't mind . . .

"Of course, Mrs. Lawson."

'Well, dear, it's those eyelashes. It's a pity for you to wear something so obviously made-up," Mother commented. "They might be all right in the evening if you have a formal affair to attend, but otherwise, it's a case of being too overdressed. Why don't you go into the bathroom and take them off so I can see how you look without them?"

Harvey looked a little mystified but determined. "Mrs. Lawson," she replied, "most people wouldn't have the courage to make such a suggestion, and I appreciate your caring enough about me to bring it up. The main problem, though, is that these *are* my eyelashes. For better or worse, they go where I go."

Mother was flabbergasted—and bested. From then on, she made sure to point out to everyone that the lashes were Harvey's own—and that they were fabulous!

Harvey and I saw each other steadily, over the objections and concern of both her mother and her brother-in-law. It was bad enough that I was Jewish, he told her, but who ever heard of a Jew without money? "He's going with you for one reason," he warned her. "He'll get what he can, then dump you for a Jewish girl."

Even then, Harvey had insight into both our lives: "Stephen was even more goal-oriented than I was, and our needs complemented one another's. Mother visualized me becoming somebody, and Stephen's mother told him he would never be anybody. Mother pushed me to be a success; Stephen's threw a curse on him by saying he'd end up a failure. We both had our eyes fixed on a goal; we both needed to prove our worthiness. We were on our way and knew we could make it with each other's support. What a great team we were!"

Yes, Harvey might be sugar, spice, and everything nice, but I learned she could handle herself under pressure and unfair tactics too. It was done with a smile, and she remained a lady. However, her walk was the tip-off. It was the most determined walk I had ever seen—feminine but with purpose. She didn't wander from point A to point B. She strode there with vigor. That same spirit carried over into every facet of her life. It would be a greater benefit in our life together than either of us could foresee.

# Chapter 7

# LOVE AND MARRIAGE

My being Jewish put no more strain on our growing relationship than did Harvey's non-Jewishness. We agreed that the only problem was that perceived by others. Religion meant almost nothing to us, so we decided to rear our children as Jews if we lived in New York since everyone I knew was Jewish. Harvey thought she should assimilate so that our children would have no ethnic disadvantages.

If we settled in the South, however, we'd rear our children as Episcopalians. I readily agreed to that since I didn't much care one way or the other. Also, I assumed it was a non-risk compromise in that we'd live in New York, anyway.

Dad died during this time, and each afternoon for the next year, I'd go to temple and say Kaddish, the mourner's prayer, in respect for his memory. This ritual had no effect on Harvey's and my relationship, and I continued secure in the belief that religion would never become an issue in our marriage.

As the months continued, however, Harvey suffered recurrent bouts of bronchitis, often severe enough to make her spend nights sitting up in bed to enable her to breathe. Her physician advised that cold air, smoking, and New York air pollution would lead to emphysema someday. The situation caused us enough concern to warrant consideration of a move to Atlanta.

There was nothing to hold us in New York except for the city's excitement and challenge. I could earn the same insurance commissions in Atlanta as in New York, I imagined, and perhaps even more. Harvey, typically, hated to turn her back on professional success. After all, she'd disciplined herself for years and longed to fulfill those personal goals.

Soon I found myself flying to Atlanta to attend our announcement party, a lovely gathering arranged by Marjory, Harvey's mother. Harvey's friends were nice and seemed genuinely interested in this Yankee she had brought south. It was springtime in Atlanta—everything in full bloom—and I fell in love with the area in no time.

The change in scene, though, brought some realizations to me. For the first time since I'd met Harvey, the religion issue made me uneasy. How could I get married in a church? I'd never knelt to pray. And they'd probably mention Jesus Christ throughout the service, which would give Mother apoplexy as she sat in the pew.

Mother was no more religious than I. Blonde and a petite five-foot-one, my blue-eyed mother didn't look a bit Jewish. Yet we *were* Jewish, and if we strayed far from our heritage, we felt uncomfortable. The bond far exceeds common worship and goes deep into cultural areas such as food, humor, homeland, types of business, history, and perceptions. All my instincts made me feel wary about marriage in a church, just as I knew Mother's did. Dad might even turn in his grave as we said our *I do*s.

At this point Harvey reminded me of our early agreement concerning religion. I'm going to have to do the changing! I thought. What a lousy deal I made. I never dreamed we'd live in Georgia—that's the Deep South!

But I had found a life's partner in Harvey. Nothing would prevent our marriage. I'd become Chinese if that's what it took for me to have her as my wife. I'd become southern *and* Episcopalian.

Though it was never spoken by either of us, an agreement was made not to tell people I was Jewish. I didn't look the part, so why subject myself even to unintentional anti-Semitism? If people asked, I'd say we belonged to All Saints, the Episcopal church where we were married. Thus we founded our marriage on a white lie and considered the situational ethics totally unimportant.

Four months later, Harvey resigned her job as a dancer and departed for Atlanta to give attention to wedding preparations. I'd join her a week before the wedding for last-minute parties and the practical work of finding an apartment, a car, and a job. Soon my departure date arrived, and I kissed Mother good-bye. She had gone from rage to relative docility by now; the idea of my being married in a church and not the temple had made life miserable at home ever since she found out.

"Mother, why are you making such a big deal out of this?" I'd argued. "You're an atheist, anyway."

"That may be true," she screamed, "but I'm a Jewish atheist, and don't you ever forget it!"

But she would join us to host the rehearsal dinner and, yes, even attend the wedding.

Thus I left behind my old life.

Harvey was a beautiful bride. I'd seen her in many shows, commercials, and other appearances, but our wedding far exceeded any of her other performances. I was a proud groom! As she stood at the back of the church, waiting for the music to begin, I glanced at Mother, sitting in the front pew. She looked old and lonely, sitting there without Dad. I felt the sting of regret that he couldn't share this day with me. Mother's face mirrored the hard life she'd experienced, and for a moment, my heart went out to her. It wasn't that I hadn't tried to express my love to her in the past, but she had never stopped fighting long enough to hear. There were always old fights to be rehashed and new battles to be waged. Mother taught me a lot about hating. She had demonstrated that hatred could be a great motivator. She herself was unable to forgive and prided herself that she never forgot. Nevertheless, in that instant on my wedding day I loved her very much and crossed to where she sat and kissed her on the cheek.

Without understanding what I'd done, I had forgiven for the first time in my life. I forgave all things past and wiped the slate clean. It was marvelous. Unfortunately, that forgiveness came from my own effort rather than the power of God's love. Therefore, it wasn't long before in the heat of conflict, I took my forgiveness back.

Harvey and I were not nervous as we said our vows. The altar kneeling was not as bad as I'd imagined, and Jesus's name was not mentioned too often. The end of the ceremony was exactly like that of a Jewish wedding: money was given to the priest in a plain white envelope to express gratitude for a lovely ceremony.

Driving toward our honeymoon at Sea Island, Georgia, we experienced a strange—and to Harvey, a significant—happening. As we traveled down the country road that approached our hotel, three white doves flew across the road and narrowly missed our windshield.

Harvey was ecstatic. While it had no significance to me, Harvey knew beyond doubt that we'd witnessed an omen of good fortune. She mentioned that the doves represented the Trinity, which was God the Father, God the Son, and God the Holy Spirit. She told me that God used a dove to impart the Holy Spirit to Jesus.

I was totally uninterested. Such conversation was wasted on a Jewish boy from New York. Some days later, however, when we'd returned from our seaside honeymoon and moved into our eighth-floor apartment, there came a sign with meaning for me.

It was the morning after our arrival, and I was savoring every moment of it. Until this time, home to me had been merely a house, a place to be avoided because it hurt too much to be there. But I truly had a home now, a place where I could be sheltered from the world's turmoil, a safe harbor. To most men, home means a woman too—his mother when he's young and his wife when he's an adult. Across the table from me was the pivotal part of my home—Harvey. Over our coffee we looked out the open window at the beautiful view. There was a delightful breeze playing around us, and minutes earlier, the rain had stopped. Now the sun broke through.

"Look, a rainbow!" we said together, looking into the distance at the most vivid arc I'd ever seen. The radiant colors were perfectly displayed.

At first, looking into the distance, we missed what was happening several inches from where we stood. Then we saw it—the rainbow's end, lodged in our window sill. The end of the rainbow! Here it was!

Like children, we stretched forth our hands and delighted to see the colors wash over our skin. For long moments we experienced the pure magic of this mystical event, something we would always remember.

"Harvey, if this is the end of the rainbow, where's the pot of gold?" I asked.

We looked at each other, now husband and wife, and smiled in agreement. The pot of gold was a myth, after all.

*Chapter 8*

# SELLING THE SIZZLE

The life insurance business wasn't going too well for me in those early days of our marriage. I hadn't wanted Harvey to work outside our home; my male ego proclaimed loudly that I should supply all her needs. But our not being able to meet the rent on time every month dictated that she help out. Harvey worked for several years until I went into business for myself.

While I starved in the insurance business, the St. Louis Hawks professional basketball team moved to Atlanta. When the team had been in town for a week, I approached the general manager about a job.

I began serving as statistician, working for press tickets, free game passes for Harvey, and ten dollars per game. I thought I'd died and gone to heaven. Within months, the general manager gave me a full-time position: director of sales. I enjoyed this job. It was a lot of fun to mention my position at cocktail parties. It certainly beat saying you sold insurance and watching people walk away. My popularity picked up considerably.

After two great years with the Hawks, I decided to form my own real estate investment firm. A close friend had left one of Atlanta's prestigious legal firms to open his own real estate investment and development enterprise, which prospered beautifully. He accepted the role of mentor in my commercial future. At first the thought of starting my own firm was a passing whim. But why not? I might not be a genius, but I hadn't met any since moving to Atlanta anyway. I was amazed at some of the people I saw who were prospering here, people who I knew would never make it in New York. It was a situation fit for an old gambler.

I instinctively knew what produced success. Impressions. Money. Thinking one step ahead of one's clients. The boy who had memorized the bar mitzvah ceremony could create investment sales pitches with far less difficulty.

I knew I could soon learn the basics of the business; I also knew that land prices in Atlanta were increasing at an unbelievable rate. Unquestionably, real estate ventures didn't lose money, ever. The issue that separated one deal from another was merely the size of the profit.

My talent consisted of selling the sizzle, not the steak. I sold "capital appreciation" and "interest write-offs" instead of real estate. It centered upon coaxing, cajoling, enticing, weaving stories, mentioning how few units were left, motivating buyers to quick decisions. It involved "sell-back provisions" that afforded buyers a false feeling of security and created a general smoke-blowing sort of existence I'd almost come to believe myself.

I did not consider myself unethical or greedy. I never sold my own property to any investment group I sponsored, and I never made a secret profit. All my investors knew I bought several units of ownership myself, which meant I'd certainly want to sell the property for as much as possible. Further, I made no additional commissions when the property eventually sold.

I considered myself one of the most reputable guys in town. A little puffing here and fudging there wouldn't affect anything as long as my investors profited in the long run. Only a jerk would say that the ends didn't justify the means.

Large commissions began to roll in. I'd never made money so easily. It was unbelievable! Harvey and I celebrated our fifth anniversary by taking a trip to the North Carolina mountains, a memorable trip because my confidence had started to build. I didn't need to feel a secret rush of envy when I looked at successful people. Now they could envy me!

I hadn't forgotten, however, those who said I'd never make it and that I'd never amount to anything—including Mother, who topped the list. Long ago I'd recognized the positive uses of such negative influences.

Many people work hard for the things that money can buy: vacations, automobiles, houses, and the like. My motivations were much more base. Any material success I ever realized—and that was considerable—arrived in direct proportion to my ability to hate. It was that hatred—simmering, controlled, and disguised—that provided the motivation and strength to work as hard as was necessary to accomplish success.

And the success felt wonderful because it vindicated Harvey's decision to marry me. She believed in me before anyone else did, and I intended her to share in my success in a most deserved fashion. The things I gave her—the beautiful home, antiques, the pleasure of designer dresses and jewelry, fine restaurants, trips, a full-length mink coat—offered tangible proof that I was no loser. Harvey was proud of me, and I took considerable pride in knowing that. Life built on a basis of performance is all right as long as you are able to perform. I could—and would continue to.

Yes, success had a price tag. I was willing to pay the tariff. I was ready, determined, and dedicated. Without realizing it, I'd called on all the help this world could afford. Satan answered, and I became a working partner with the demons of manipulation and deception. What a team we made!

Chapter 9

# LOVE AND MONEY

losing followed closing, and I headed for more success than I'd ever dreamed of attaining. Harvey no longer had to work. Instead, we could take trips to Bermuda and other lovely places, buying beautiful clothes before and during each journey. Two new Mercedes-Benz automobiles ornamented our driveway. We often attended the Florida racetracks to watch our thoroughbreds run. We ate in the very best restaurants, and often. Our lives were changing drastically; Harvey's as much as mine. Harvey described our lives at this time: "Stephen was so sure of himself, confident, bright, and tenacious. I knew I could trust him with my very life. I loved to work with him on any project, but I excelled at being Mrs. Stephen P. Lawson. *President* or *chairman* always came after my name when it appeared in newspaper pictures or articles documenting our life.

"I was a leader in several of the art organizations in town, receiving a great deal of attention and recognition for my capabilities. I was a tireless worker in the community, which might be expected of the youngest president of a major arts organization. I was pictured with the mayor and the governor for my efforts as a creative fund raiser. I presented silver cups at horse shows and received awards and plaques for my efforts and achievements.

"While I was a star in the volunteer community, Stephen attained success as one of the five largest privately owned real estate investment firms in Atlanta. We were a sought-after couple—on the go seven days a week, the phones constantly ringing. I kept saying yes to volunteer commitments because these tasks provided me solid feelings of worthiness and power. My decisions meant something. I attained a high profile in the volunteer community."

The thing that separated me from others in the Atlanta real estate syndication market was that I majored in people, not land. "You know, Bob," I'd say, "a fringe benefit of my business is that I meet so many people, including some I really like. I sure would like the girls to have an opportunity to meet one another, and I was thinking, I have four tickets to the basketball game this Thursday evening. Why don't we all plan to go? Let's get a bite to eat at the Omni Club beforehand."

I operated from a kind of cunning self-deception. Knowing that all of us want to be loved, I resolved to "love" my clients and shower them with thoughtfulness and generosity. Actually, it wasn't love at all but a new form of my old manipulative habits, one so subtle that even I didn't recognize it.

Sometimes Harvey and I went out sixteen evenings straight, entertaining potential investors. Not all invested with my firm, of course, but 90 percent did.

What's more, these investors referred me to others. Referrals, by and large, come from people who consider you a friend, and I was accumulating more "friends" than anyone else in town.

My attorneys were friends too—or at least one of them was. He had opened his own firm, specializing in criminal law, several years before. Recently he had taken a partner. I recall a meeting at Hilton Head Island to discuss their representing me in the formation of land syndications.

They acknowledged knowing nothing about real estate but agreed to learn and represent me because of the sizable fees I'd generate.

Life was a piece of cake, and everything Mother had told me about making money was true: "Remember, Steve, you're nothing without money. A buck is your best friend." In truth, Mother never taught me the value of a dollar; she taught me the value of $100,000.

And she appeared to be right. Harvey and I were becoming more and more in demand. I was successful enough that people were laughing harder at my stories. Even my sister's husband, Arthur, who was the CEO of a large firm in New York invested with the kid brother who was taking the world by storm down there in Atlanta.

Marjory, my mother-in-law, claimed I was a genius. I secretly admired her discernment. My office had to be enlarged in order to house a person of my intelligence, kindness, and shrinking humility. Class A personalities asked for my opinions about things.

One Monday morning my secretary called to say she'd be late, and I found myself alone, contemplating a conversation Harvey and I had had the evening before.

"Stephen, I have a funny feeling, and it's important that we discuss it."

"Of course, honey. What is it?"

"There's no one in the world happier about your— our—success than I am. I enjoy being the wife of a man who's successful, and I love being able to do all the things we dreamed of doing, but . . ."

"But what?"

"Well, the truth is, something is missing."

"What do you mean?"

"I don't know. . . . Remember when you worked at the Atlanta Hawks' office, and we'd go down after dinner, and I'd help you with a lot of things because you didn't have a secretary?"

"Yeah, I sure do. We were both working, and our biggest project was paying off the Standard Oil bill so they'd return our credit card."

Harvey laughed a little at the recollection. "Honey, that's what I mean when I said something is missing. Somehow we don't have the same satisfaction we seemed to have back then."

Harvey's comments didn't disturb me; they left me more curious than anything else. Our relationship was as good as ever. True, we worked very hard, but only so we could enjoy things together.

If I had been honest, though, I would have told Harvey that I also felt something was missing. Despite the money I was making, I still couldn't seem to buy the respect of those I most wanted to impress—the ones with negative predetermined opinions of me—some family members, several friends in New York, and of course, Mother.

I worked so hard to show them they were wrong about me but still hadn't obtained the thrill which I felt entitled. Money wasn't turning out to be the great reward I had expected.

Each month I sent Mother $400 to help meet her monthly obligations, and the only satisfaction it gave me was to see her signature on the cashed checks. Actually, she never needed the money as much as I needed to send it. I needed her to see how well I was doing and how wrong she had been about me. It was my way of rubbing her nose in it on a thirty-day basis.

But that was not my main problem. I knew that I was a fraud, that I was not the financial mind I purported to be in the sales pitches I was forever giving. Actually, I was no smarter than when I had struggled in the insurance business; I was merely more calculating and brazen.

I was a real gunslinger, and no one seemed to see it but me. I also felt somewhat awkward about the money I was making. Based on the effort expended, I had to be earning more money per ounce of effort than anyone else in the world.

I couldn't philosophize long that day as I pondered my conversation with Harvey and faced momentarily my own moral discomforts. I had been rich, and I had been poor, and as a comedian once said, "Rich is better."

There was a bigger problem that needed my attention at that time. I'd sponsored an investment earlier and collected all the monies required for closing by getting it fully subscribed. The problem was, I had to pay my bookmaker for my accumulated gambling losses. So I took money from the limited-partnership account.

At first I took only the amount of the commission I was due to earn. Advancing commissions before the closing was wrong enough, but I did not stop there. Later I took substantially more. I was raised on a New York code of ethics that was true everywhere: either pay your bookie on time or assume, most correctly, that you had wished you had. When closing time arrived, I lacked funds needed to complete the property purchase. Of course I planned to pay it all back when my luck changed next week.

What could I do? *Obviously I had to obtain an extension until I was able to close.* I bought an extra thirty days by taking another $5,000 from the limited-partnership account.

In all, I obtained three extensions but was unable to negotiate a fourth. *How could I get out of this one?*

"Right, Sam,*" I lied to an investor, "we had the closing yesterday, and I think there's already someone interested in buying this property from us. The thing is, we need to hold it for six months to qualify for the capital-gains treatment."

Alone in my air-conditioned office, I began to sweat with the effort it took to keep my voice casual, neither hurried nor loud, while I maneuvered myself out of a dangerously tight corner with an investor who wouldn't get off the phone.

"How much is he talking about? Well, I'm looking at getting our original investment back with about a 40 percent profit! That's 80 percent if you figure it on an annual basis. . . . That's right, Sam, we could have held it longer, but as Dad used to say, 'You can't go broke taking a profit.'" At last he hung up. I mopped the sweat off my face and told my heart to stop pounding. I didn't have their money, and they didn't have an investment. I'd just sold Sam a bunch of hot air but had bought myself some time. Given six months, I'd get out of this mess. Of course, had I told Sam the truth, I could have been put out of business. I was smart enough to know that my conduct was criminal. I knew I had to come up with some gambling winnings or earn some new commissions. Either way, I kept telling myself, *No problem*.

Within six months I accomplished what I'd set out to do. Each investor received back his original investment plus a 40 percent cash profit, which came directly from my pocket.

I considered the matter closed—expensively closed, but closed. For the first time in over eight months I was able to take a deep breath without trembling.

I knew gambling had me in its hold, and I wanted to stop or at least cut back. Unfortunately, I'd see bargains I couldn't pass up without a heavy bet. By now, my bookmaker was far ahead of me. I had to make substantial bets if I was to have any prospect of getting my money back. Now I was betting just to break even.

Harvey had become aware that I was betting, but she had no idea of the amounts involved. We had arguments from time to time when she caught me red-handed—and red-faced—talking to my bookmaker on the telephone.

I had developed an inexhaustible tolerance for a dark and secretive way of life. Winnings could never change my life. I had reached a point where my wants and desires couldn't keep pace with my earning capacity. When I lost, I had to rendezvous with the bookmaker to pay off my debts. Every expression and word out of his mouth mocked me. Drawing large sums of cash out of the bank made me feel dirty and uneasy; I had to endure the cute remarks from a bank teller who asked if I were paying a kidnapper later in the day.

But in spite of all this, I would tell Harvey I had to leave the house for a few minutes to get a newspaper or to buy something at the store—so that I could call the bookie from a phone booth. The line could be busy for twenty minutes at a time, and in the winter, the temperature might be twenty degrees with a wind-chill factor of minus three. But I kept dialing until the line was free. I returned home and wouldn't leave the television set. Weekends revolved around the games. Sometimes I was euphoric, but most of the time my feelings were cluttered junctions of fury, dismay, anger, and frustration. At all times, I attempted to conceal my life. Gambling was a morbid compulsion—something I would never have let my worst enemy do to me.

Nothing could make me stop. Though I loved Harvey more than anything else in the world, that love couldn't force me to stop. Betting continued. Losing continued. Never did I stop to realize that I was addicted, and the stakes were higher than I could imagine: Harvey, our marriage, our way of life.

Meanwhile, certain investors proved helpful in the area of cash flow. This group invested with me each time I had an offering. Since many closings were so far in the future, I sold them on the idea that it was silly to have all their savings sitting in credit unions earning a modest interest. I offered these investors an opportunity to pool their money with others in Certificates of Deposit I was purchasing at a much higher yield. Naturally, that certain group decided to take advantage of such a good idea. But there were no Certificates of Deposit nor would there ever be.

They're getting the interest they seek, I rationalized. I'll pay it out of my commissions. Since they invest with me so regularly anyway, I'm doing no more than advancing myself what would be future commissions.

The only problem with this smooth scheme was that my actions were morally wrong. And as I would eventually find out, I would be found criminally accountable also.

# Chapter 10

# THE APPROACHING STORM

Harvey and I approached 1974 from two distinctly different perspectives. For me, there was the relief of knowing I'd weathered the past year and all its problems. Not only had I pulled my business out of its troubles, but I'd earned more than half a million dollars and expected the coming year to be even better. (To put those 1972 earnings in better perspective, the most prestigious estate in Atlanta sold for $300,000. That same residence in 1992 sold for 3.5 million.)

Also, I was cleaning up my act somewhat. I had cut way back on my betting and had hired a CPA firm to put my books in order and closely monitor me in the future by setting up accounts I couldn't invade. I'd made a full disclosure of my past year's dealings and believed they'd provide a good check on my activities.

I knew I'd walked into the lion's den the year before and was lucky I'd come out alive. I wouldn't have that happen again. Next time I might not survive!

Harvey, meanwhile, had been expecting our first child in late January. It had been a wonderful pregnancy, and we looked forward to becoming parents. We had waited eight years to start a family, and it seemed our timing was perfect. Harvey expressed it this way: "I wanted to slow down long enough to have a family, and while I was pregnant, my first feelings of fear surfaced. We had everything—all the money anyone could use, a beautiful home, cars, clothes, jewelry, and the invitation I had worked so hard to attain: I was invited into the Junior League.

"I was on a cloud for a while, but then that feeling of, *Is this all there is?* became prominent. I shared my feelings with Stephen more than once and found myself crying for several days. We had worked so hard to achieve all this, but now that I was slowing down and had time for reflection, it didn't look so great. Stephen assured me my feelings were just hormonal."

Our baby arrived on the fifth of February. We called our new son Blake. At home, our happiness scale peaked when Blake came into our lives. At work, the curve began to nose dive. My troubles began to take shape soon into 1974, with a phone call from my accountants.

"I know you want to give those fellows your business," my accountants said, "but they can get you into more trouble than you dream. We represent a lot of men in your industry and are familiar with the sort of legal work you require. You've simply got to retain attorneys who specialize in securities." I'd heeded their advice and made several changes in my business, including the area of my legal representation.

Previously, one of the accountants phoned to warn me to be sure to have my then attorneys file the limited-partnership paperwork concerning my 1973 closings by April 1, 1974. "Steve, did you have them file with the state securities office?"

"Of course. You reminded me months ago, and I've reminded them several times. They assured me they'd take care of it."

"That's good, because it's quite a problem if they don't. Let's get a Photostat of those documents from their files."

At that point, we learned that the prepared documents never had been filed with the state. Georgia securities laws had changed, meanwhile, and there was no saving clause that would allow a late filing. When my former attorneys belatedly attempted to file, the answer was no.

The office of my former attorneys was in the same building as my office. We called a meeting that included my accountants and new attorneys with the intent to coordinate an effort and to work together. After all, mistakes are mistakes. My former attorneys had already consulted one of the most prestigious law firms in town. Battle lines had been drawn. My former attorneys were starting to circle the wagons.

"Okay, perhaps we should have filed the papers prior to April 1. But if all the things we now know about Steve were known to us before, we would have had to make some kind of disclosure, and he wouldn't have been able to put a deal together, anyway."

"Andy,* what are you talking about?" I shouted.

"You know full well what I'm talking about. You're not going to take me down the drain with you! I had no idea you were invading those limited-partnership accounts prior to the closing."

"Why, you creep! Don't hand me that garbage! You did know about it. You knew I took it out of the partnership accounts. You needed me to pay your closing fees in advance because your lack of cash flow was going to put you under without my help! The advances were from the limited-partnership accounts. And you mean to tell me you had no idea where the money kept coming from to extend the time on that aborted Cherokee deal? The checks I gave the seller for the extensions came from the partnership account, and you were the one who gave it to him."

"Lawson, you're crazy, and I don't know what you're talking about. Let's get one thing straight—your blood isn't on my hands. Whatever happens to you, you've brought it all on yourself without any help from me! Now get out of my office!"

"Yeah, I'll get out all right!" I fumed. "The stink around here is making me sick. You've always been a sanctimonious jerk, Andy, but I'll tell you one thing—if this is going to end up being a bloodbath, you're going to get as bloody as I get."

My new attorneys spelled it out for me. I did have a problem, though at that time, I could see only the tip of the iceberg. Since I did not fall under the private-placement exemption a proper and timely filing would have afforded, I now came under the Federal Securities Act that required the sort of documentation and disclosure I was not required to give under a private placement.

"Listen," I said. "It wasn't even my mistake. Surely they'll understand if we go to them and explain."

"True," my lawyers advised me, "but they'd demand you make a full offering circular of every investment you closed and give the investors a copy."

"It will be expensive and a pain in the neck, but that's okay," I replied.

"Then you have to offer them a chance to rescind their investment if they wish. Do you have money available to repay all who might like to get out?"

Of course I didn't. There was no way I could offer all those investors a chance to pull out of their investments. Of the monies collected, most went to the sellers at closing. Legal fees had also been paid. I shook my head.

"Stephen, you really have a problem," they offered soberly.

I had two options, it appeared, and neither was pleasant. First, I could pretend I didn't have a problem at all; perhaps nothing would come of my former attorneys' oversight. That was potentially dangerous, however, in that any investor who wanted out and consulted an attorney might end up letting all the investors know they were entitled to a rescission of their investment. A real estate recession had just begun in Atlanta, and investors might have leapt at such an opportunity.

My other option was to take the bold approach: simply go to the Securities and Exchange Commission (SEC), and confess the error. I was encouraged to think that would impress the Commission and that I would receive merely a slap on the wrist.

I decided to take the second approach, and my attorneys helped me prepare a disclosure document for the SEC. I felt uncomfortable signing it since it placed in writing the candid facts about the aborted closing and payback along with facts concerning the Certificate of Deposit monies. I signed it and took it to the SEC, where I immediately knew I was in trouble. My heart sank as I realized that these officials did not deal in wrist slapping but were serious as a heart attack about their intent to investigate my firm's irregular use of clients' monies.

Despite my years of experience in explaining my way out of tight places, I had no desire to try to bluff or manipulate. The SEC investigated my firm for more than half a year with my full cooperation and disclosure of all requested facts. Meanwhile, my new attorneys advised me not to promote any other land ventures. My former attorneys were given good advice when told to get out of my boat. It was developing more leaks than I could begin to plug.

At last, on December 1, I received a phone call from the Commission. They'd received an order from Washington about me and my firm. The action would be limited to my signing a civil consent order saying I'd violate no security laws in the future.

My heart sang. Just a slap on the wrist, after all. Finally, the nightmare was over, and I could resume my business. I signed the papers, kept a copy for myself, and bade the SEC good-bye.

The next morning, as I read my newspaper, the bottom dropped out of my personal world. A news story and headlines related that Stephen P. Lawson and Cambridge Capital Corporation had signed a consent order after admitting to fraud and that a special fiscal agent of the court would run the affairs of the various partnerships.

As I read further, to my horror, I saw the story included details of my Certificates of Deposit scheme and details of the aborted land closing. Nowhere did it mention that these people had been paid back at a handsome profit.

As quickly as my morning newspaper slid from my fingers, I realized I was out of business.

Though my business was effectively destroyed, it took months for it to die. For the remainder of that year and the next, I worked with the special fiscal agent as investor meetings were held. Our investors had totally lost confidence and looked upon me as a "smoothie" who had taken their hard-earned money.

With each month that passed, my props began to go—the beautiful cars and elegant office, my public image, the bank accounts, our clients, my "friends," even those I had "loved" and lavishly entertained.

One investor approached me angrily, yelling that I could take his wife, but how dare I take his money! A close friend, more honest and direct, put it this way: "Steve, until this entire episode is behind you, I don't think we should see each other anymore."

I shouldn't be surprised at this sort of thing, I told myself. Mother was right. A dollar really is your best friend when all is said and done.

In the end, all the investment groups went under, and I had been the single largest investor. I was broke and out of business. There was no reason to have an office when there were no investors, and there was no use having overhead when there was no way to pay the bills.

The first thing I did upon coming to this realization was to visit Don Patterson at the Edwards Baking company. Aside from wanting to interview for a position there, I was drawn to speak to Don for reasons I couldn't readily explain.

He had been an investor of mine and had referred others to me. All of them had lost money. Still, for some reason, I approached Don with my problems, somehow knowing he'd be responsive. Also, I wanted him to know how sorry I was to have caused him so many problems. I was genuinely sorry for Don's losses.

Amazingly, Don hadn't seen the paper and knew nothing. He received the news without much display of emotion considering he'd just learned that some $25,000 of his investments had gone down the tubes. I explained that I was broke and needed a job.

"How is Harvey? How's she taking all this?" Don asked. Then he reached into his desk drawer and wrote me a check for $5,000. "Steve, I hope this will help. You can pay me someday when you're able. Meantime, I'll set up some appointments for you here, though I can't guarantee you a position."

His attitude totally disarmed me. The hurts I'd sustained from other friends fled from my memory as I contemplated Don's calm and compassionate demeanor.

As I drove away, I tried to figure him out. During all our married life, Harvey and I had known Don and Patti, and although we regularly swapped dinner invitations, you could hardly call us close friends. They made no bones about Christ being the center of their home. They acted, to my notion, like typical Bible Belt people, the sort who seem to have lived their lives without hatred, jealousy, or trauma and have always had an excellent relationship with parents who adore them and would be offended if they didn't show up for Sunday brunch at the club. As I saw it, the God they thought was so marvelous must also be the same one who created acne, bad breath, and athlete's foot and caused your teeth to fall out of your head during old age.

At home, Harvey was equally impressed. That day she and I sat alone and talked a long time about the concerns that filled our life.

"We're about to go through some rough times," I told my wife. "I can remember when my folks went through some similar trials."

Through my mind's eye, I saw a montage of old horror scenes—Mother, contorted with fear, and my aging father, demoralized and hopeless, berating one another and at last turning on me. I panicked at the thought that my own adult life would mirror that of my parents. The unbearable things Mother had said to my father she had also said to me. He had died at last and gotten beyond the effect of those words— which at that moment were being revived. I tried to convey to Harvey the video replay that was going on inside me.

"Harvey, we must make a pledge to one another to be kind to each other at all times. Honey, I couldn't stand it if you were to become to me what Mother ended up being to my dad."

Harvey assured me. There were to be no recriminations. Whatever needed doing—even returning to work and leaving her fourteen-month-old baby—she did willingly and with a beautiful spirit.

Lawsuits started pouring in. Each evening the doorbell rang, and the marshal served us with more. In all, I was to receive some $600,000 worth of lawsuits from former investors who sought rescission of their investments and return of all money invested, due to the missed filing date.

*Missed filing date?* I recognized that point as being merely a legal ruse. Each of these suits, I persuaded myself, indicated my clients' belief in me; they were lining up with me against my attorneys.

In every case, as I answered the suits, I brought my former attorneys in as third-party defendants. My posture was that if the investors held valid assumptions that I owed them money, it was due to my attorneys' malpractice. And attorneys have malpractice insurance. This "deep pocket" was what the investors were after.

I viewed these suits as a great opportunity for vindication. Should my attorneys be judged at fault by the legal process they served, I would consider that the ultimate vindication. I also sued my former attorneys for malpractice and punitive damages in excess of a million dollars. I believed, as did many others, that I had to win. It was an open-and-shut case.

For years we were to wage battle, and for years, I was to hate with all my heart. It would take nearly five years for me to understand that I must admit my own guilt and accept responsibility for my own actions.

Meanwhile, I clung to the belief that I could not possibly lose my lawsuits. Even if I did, however, my former attorneys would see their practice destroyed by rumors and idle talk—exactly as my business had been. They too depended upon referrals. Soon they'd be hurting financially.

They would learn, as I had, that trying to stop a rumor was like trying to un-ring a bell.

I believed my hatred was justified. Not only had the attorneys erred initially in not filing the papers, but now they blamed me entirely. They claimed to know nothing about my past actions (such as comingled funds), though in fact, they did. They stonewalled and lied, and I viewed their conduct as despicable.

While I devoted myself single-mindedly to my hatred, Harvey dealt with other, more immediate realities. I had no job and couldn't get one. Day by day, our prospects grew more nightmarish. As Harvey relates, "We had no business, no source of income; our investments were lost, the savings wiped out. We were jobless and without hope of any kind. I would wake in the night in a sweat, heart pounding, sure that I was having a nightmare, then remember that we were living a nightmare. It was obvious that I would have to go back to work—and immediately."

As I lost myself in hatred, Harvey was submerged in pain. Her notes reflect our general turmoil: "I hadn't lost only the material things. I was cut off from the very things that had given me my sense of identity and worthiness. Additionally, I had put all my energy, faith, and trust in Stephen. I had backed a winner, and now he had lost—and lost big. It wasn't just the loss of money; we had lost our acceptability.

"I perceived condemnation that was both real and imagined. I didn't want to go anywhere; I was sure even the grocery store manager had read the awful things about us in the newspapers. Certainly I couldn't go to any volunteer meetings. I even felt squeamish about walking the dog or seeing people in our condominium association."

Harvey found a job and returned to work. I learned that no one wants to hire a person with lawsuits pending, and after countless interviews I settled into the only job I could find—that of househusband in our own home.

It became my special time to be with Blake, a time few fathers ever experience. I believe the special bond between Blake and me was formed at that time.

Yes, there were advantages, but after two years in limbo, I knew I needed to go back to work, and I needed it desperately.

So when Jeff,* a former investor, phoned and wanted to get together, I found myself quite receptive.

# Chapter 11

# UNDERCOVER WORK

There have been some forthright conversations in my life but none quite as forthright as the one with Jeff that afternoon. Jeff was a successful physician in the greater Atlanta area. I could see that he intended to capitalize on my misfortune by helping me return to business, becoming my silent partner, and making a handsome profit for himself.

He had a simple plan. He knew a great number of physicians out of state, mostly in the Carolinas and in Florida. He'd send me to see them with rave reviews, declare he intended to become a principal investor in the land under discussion, and encourage their participation. Since they were out of state, they'd know nothing about me and my problems. We were confident that my salesmanship could handle potential objections of investing in Atlanta rather than in their own locales.

Never mind ethics. Strong hatred for my former attorneys and all others who were accessories to my downfall made me jump at Jeff's suggestions. I was hungry and hurting.

Jeff's plan, motivated by greed and greased by deception, tied in with my own strong needs and motivations.

It had been more than two years since I'd made a living. My househusband duties had reached the point of diminishing returns and made it easy for me to justify violating my consent order. After all, hadn't my attorneys been the ones at fault? Despite that, it was *my* family who suffered. I'd show them; I'd make a successful comeback.

I had learned a great deal about the laws concerning securities (much more than I'd ever wanted to know, actually). I realized I was violating my consent order in the most basic way by not providing potential investors with full disclosure. Full disclosure would dictate that I tell them all about the SEC action and the lawsuits pending, not to mention other negative details. The trouble was, such disclosure would mean I'd sell no units of ownership.

The answer? I had someone else serve as general partner, thus concealing from the securities authorities my involvements with these investments. The offering circulars sent to the state securities office in Atlanta were approved without delay. I honestly believed my actions would go undetected.

Armed with introductions that wouldn't fail, I drove to Florida to start a prolonged selling trip. I met many nice people who bought what they saw and who invested willingly. I received their money with confidence that the investments were sound and that they'd eventually produce handsome profits. The land was purchased, and I rationalized that the lack of disclosure to which these investors were entitled made no difference whatever since they were going to make money.

I was getting back on my feet, making money again. I had leased a Mercedes-Benz so that the image of prosperity would be transmitted to any prospective investors. I had even begun to make an impression on myself. I believed I was planting seeds for an even more prosperous future than before.

From today's perspective, however, I see that God was allowing me those last yards of line, and I was playing myself out. I was like a fish that had been hooked and fighting, unable to pull free, panicked and desperate and— using every last ounce of energy—finally must yield and is pulled into the boat, exhausted.

Harvey struggled in her thoughts: "It was good to see Stephen busy again. It was more than the fact he was putting together the finances of our life; he was the guy who I could truly depend on to overcome any obstacle—the sort of person described by the saying "When life hands you a lemon, make lemonade." I was proud of him. Yet something deep inside told me that this was only temporary.

"I couldn't help but remember the large beetle I had observed while sitting on a park bench one day. Somehow it had landed on its back and was using every bit of energy to right itself, knowing, I guess, that it would die in its present state. After ten minutes passed it turned over and started heading off the pavement to the grassy area. At that moment a child ran by and stepped on the beetle, killing it instantly. The child ran off, never knowing what had happened and the role she had played as terminator in that bug's life. I could only hope that somehow we wouldn't be like that bug—working so hard to survive only to have someone squash us.

"I couldn't enjoy Stephen's comeback in the way I had shared in his original successes. *What was the matter? Time would tell*, I guessed."

I had left Palm Beach and was headed toward Lakeland, Florida. Previously I had met several doctors at a well-known clinic, and we were to meet again that afternoon. It was a beautiful day, and the road stretched in front of me like a ribbon for as far as I could see.

My thoughts, as usual, centered on my former attorneys, and I hoped it was true that "every turkey had its Thanksgiving." I contemplated the progress of the lawsuits and the upcoming deposition and then turned my full attention to hating them. The venom in my heart erupted through my body, and I was absolutely obsessed by the idea of coming up with a new way to do to them what they had done to me.

I turned on the radio and then put in a musical tape. I leaned back in the seat and tried to relax. My former attorneys might be worthy of all the emotional effort I was expending, but the effort was sapping and made me half-crazy every time I directed thought to it.

Suddenly, the loneliness was upon me. I hadn't experienced it since having met Harvey some eleven years ago. As with the wind, I had no idea where it had come from, but it had returned—and the torment it produced was instantaneous.

These feelings of loneliness were incredible, and they came at the craziest times. I could have understood having those kinds of emotions when I was alone or during moments of sadness or disappointment. But it was never depression; it was a feeling of being totally alone in life without anyone caring about me or loving me. And with it came the desperate, oppressive feeling that there was absolutely no hope of change or recovery.

It always came without warning. One minute I was fine, the next, consumed by the sense of total alienation and would remain so for the next few days. I could be the life of a party (as I often was) and on the spot become the most desolate person in the room. My outward persona never changed since I was a great actor and could carry on for the entire evening as though nothing were wrong. But something *was* wrong—everything was wrong.

Had I possessed the keys to the kingdom of heaven itself, I would have given them up in a New York minute in order to relieve that loneliness permanently.

In earlier years I had considered that part of it had to do with being single—having no roots or place to really belong. But this was no longer the case; I had a wife who was enviously beautiful, charming, and loving. *Why this onslaught of feelings now?*

I no longer heard the tape player, and I could hardly drive the car. Instead of driving it with confidence, I was merely aiming the car in an attempt to keep it on the road. There were no other cars within sight, and the road was as straight as an arrow. Nevertheless, all coordination had deserted me, and fear for my life encompassed me. Despite the emotional storm raging within, I continued to drive. Every hurt, bad experience, and pathos I had known filled these moments of loneliness.

At that point God was starting to take the initiative in bringing me to himself. For some reason, at that moment, I looked up over the horizon into the clouds and said, "Jesus, please help me. I can do anything on my own, but I can't handle these feelings of loneliness, and I ask you to take them from me." Without realizing it, I had admitted that Jesus was Lord and that he was fully capable of taking my pain from me if I asked. At that time, spiritual discernment was beyond me. All I knew was that, within an instant, the loneliness had departed. Not only had it departed, but I felt better than I had in years. I had been road weary, having been away from home for about two weeks. Now it was as if I had just had a marvelous night's sleep and awoke to a hot shower. I felt fresh—invigorated. When a person has been met at the very point of his need, it tends to grab his attention. The experience I have just related might not seem like a miracle to some, but it certainly qualified as one in my view.

My meetings in Lakeland concluded successfully. I drove on to Gainesville and arrived in the early evening. I hadn't told anyone about my experience yet, so I called Harvey.

"You won't believe what happened to me on the road today," I began. The event unfolded, and strangely, there wasn't much of a response on the other end of the phone.

"Honey, how interesting. Are you feeling okay now?" She said, changing the subject.

"Yeah, I feel fine."

I got off the phone with Harvey and sat on the edge of the bed. It hadn't been a very satisfying conversation. Who could I share it with who might see the significance in what happened like I did—whatever it was?

*Of course. The Pattersons.* I smiled and dialed the number. Patti's cheerful voice flooded my ear.

"Hi, Patti. It's Steve Lawson."

"Hi, Steve! How are you?" Patti always has had a knack for making a person feel that she has been sitting by the phone waiting for their call.

I explained where I was, that I was on business, but something had happened I had to tell them about. "I think I had a religious experience. It was the darnedest thing that ever happened in my entire life."

She was definitely interested. I related what had happened, giving her some background on my bouts of severe loneliness. The only thing I didn't admit was how unusual it was for me to have uttered Jesus's name. The Pattersons didn't know I was Jewish any more than anyone in my southern circle of acquaintances.

"Oh, Steve, that's wonderful!"

"What do you make of it?" I asked.

"I don't know other than to say that I think the Lord is trying to tell you he loves you."

This was a typical Patti Patterson response. All the times before her religious jargon had turned me off completely. But it didn't seem to bother me so much this time. Then she asked if we could pray. I said I didn't mind, more to be polite than anything else. And so she prayed—a prayer I only half listened to. Hidden in this prayer, it seemed that she was delicately preaching a message to me. Finally, she finished, and we hung up. *She's a religious flake,* I thought.

*She said that Don would still be at the office. He'll have some straight talk for me.* I phoned him, and we talked for about fifteen minutes. It was obvious that somehow Patti had tipped him off to our conversation, because he didn't seem at all surprised, and his answers were much the same as hers. But I knew that they couldn't have talked, because I had dialed him directly after speaking with her and had reached him without delay.

After our conversation, I came across a *Good News for Modern Man* Bible sitting on the table next to the phone. On the cover there was an explanation that the Bible was a gift from the people at Days Inn and an invitation for me to take it with me when I left.

I praise God today not only for the ministry of that company that placed a Bible in each room but also that it was an easy-to-understand version. I picked up the Bible and quickly looked through it. It was a New Testament. *This is the one with Jesus all through it, the Testament that Jews don't acknowledge. Hmmm.* I sat down in a chair and started to read at the beginning—Matthew.

"This is the genealogy of Jesus Christ. . . ."

"Boy, it doesn't take them long to get into it, does it!" I said laughingly. I closed the book, leaving my fingers by the page I had started.

"Dear God," I prayed as best I knew how, "if you are really who you say you are, and Jesus is really who he said he was, and if this book is really your inspired Word, well . . . then I'm going to commit myself to reading it. But the rest is up to you. Amen." After all, it was honest to let him know where I stood.

I leaned back, got comfortable, and started reading the book. I knew nothing at all about Jesus and had never been in church to hear the gospel, much less read any Scripture. I didn't even realize what a Gospel was, much less that there were four or what they were about or who they were written to or by.

After a while I realized for a person who never read much, I had been totally engrossed in reading the Bible for three hours. I was starving. I got in the car and headed for a nearby restaurant. I would read, question, and consider Jesus for the next two years before I asked him into my heart. But the journey that would change my life had begun—and somehow I knew I was much like the person Jesus had met on the path who had been blind from birth. Jesus had touched him, and he was never the same. When questioned, the man said that a man had done it. Later he was to say that Jesus was a prophet. Later still he would call him Lord. Yes, something had happened on that road, like it or not. But maybe I was making too much of it. At that point all I knew was that I was going to continue to read that Bible as soon as I returned from dinner.

On Friday afternoon, following my road experience, I hurried toward Atlanta and the people I loved most— Harvey and Blake. All that travel was getting old. When I got honest with myself, I had to admit that doing business on the sly held little satisfaction. Success was hollow. It was great to pay the bills again, true, but apart from that, the work generated very little personal satisfaction. I couldn't help but remember the old days of additional cash back in New York.

I'd make some money with the bookmaker but couldn't let any of it show because of my folks. Now I had to adopt a low profile because of the SEC and unresolved lawsuits from former investors. History had repeated itself.

That evening, Tim & Alice Jones* arrived for dinner. They are such comfortable people, and we always enjoyed being in their company. I thought that Harvey's choice of dinner and friends, in honor of my first night back, was wonderful. "Say, Tim, did Harvey mention what happened to me on the road this week?" I asked.

"No, what do you mean?"

"I was driving between Palm Beach and Lakeland," the story began. Some twenty minutes later, I'd recounted it all. Tim had interrupted several times to exclaim, "You don't say!" and Alice had remarked, "Oh, my word." All was silent at the other end of the table, however.

Harvey had heard the story before, of course. She had been silent when I told it by telephone, but now I was with her and could read her face and mood. It was clear that she wanted to change the subject, and she managed to do so in short order.

The following week I shared my Florida experience with several other couples, and each time Harvey added nothing but a quiet display of annoyance. After I'd related the story for perhaps the fourth time, she could stand it no longer.

"Listen, Stephen," she warned me one evening as we prepared for bed, "I've had it with this Jesus stuff."

"What are you talking about?" I queried.

"You know, that road story you keep telling. I've absolutely had it, and I want to tell you, mister, that if you don't stop this Jesus business, I'm going to wring your neck."

She wasn't kidding. You could tell by the way she said it that the conversation was closed. There was nothing left to discuss, and if I were smart, I'd agree with her and never tell that story again. Any time Harvey injects the word "mister" into a sentence, you know you're skating on very thin ice. But I wasn't that smart.

"Can I please ask what in the world you're talking about?" I asked.

"Look, I think it's absurd that a Jewish man is sitting at a dinner table, night after night, talking about Jesus Christ and what happened to him on the road. Aside from that, you and I have always been best friends, and I'm not going to risk your becoming a religious fanatic like the Pattersons."

"Harvey, I think you've lost your mind! I know I'm Jewish, and if you think I'm going to become a Jesus freak, then you're crazier than I ever thought you could get."

"Then why do you bring it up so often, and why are you starting to read the Bible?"

"First of all, honey, I've never read it before," I said. "All of our Atlanta friends are gentiles, and I'm curious to know their beliefs. I'd like to have some background so I don't sound as stupid in conversation as they do sometimes when they refer to Jews."

"Are you sure that's it?"

"Of course. I can't see why you'd even consider me a prospect for this stuff," I reassured her, believing every word I said. "It isn't compatible for me as a Jew, and I wouldn't desecrate Dad's memory for anything. You know that. Also, I wouldn't say the secret way I'm going about making a living is something I care to sit down and discuss with God!"

We both laughed, and the tension was broken.

Harvey, however, continued to turn to me from time to time, saying in her way that she had reached the end of her inner resources. She described it this way: "I threw myself into my job and let it overcome and possess me. While Stephen was obsessed with legalities, hatred for his former attorneys, and the need for justification at any cost, I became obsessive-compulsive about my work.

"Desperately lonely in that job, alienated and cast aside from old friends, and without the time, desire, or opportunity to develop new ones, I shared all my needs and concerns with Stephen. I told him how lonely and lost I was. I told him I felt like a spent piece of elastic; I couldn't spring back anymore.

"Stephen tried to help. It isn't that he wouldn't; he couldn't. I couldn't listen to the constant talk regarding the legalities, and Stephen couldn't talk about anything else. We went through the motions of sharing and talking as we always had done, but neither of us could hear the other's cry for help.

"We were hopelessly lost, trying to control our own lives, which were destined for disaster, using all the old techniques we had used successfully in the past but now no longer worked."

My phone calls to Patti and Don had jolted them both into action on my behalf. Harvey and I became permanent fixtures on the prayer list posted on Patti's refrigerator door.

Books began appearing in our mailbox, such as *Evidence That Demands a Verdict,* though we never saw them placed there. Frankly, I found the books quite interesting and began to phone Don fairly often to ask questions about this point or that.

The books, phone calls, questions, and study continued on an irregular basis for about two years. Once Don had me meet him at his office so I could meet his prayer partner, who Don claimed could answer some of my tougher questions.

I read those books faithfully, almost every night. Occasionally I missed one evening's reading because I couldn't find the books—and knew Harvey had hidden them again. Or if she hadn't hidden them, they certainly weren't in the same place twice.

The deposition with my former attorneys took place in the offices of one of Atlanta's leading law firms. It looked like a bar convention. Every lawyer representing clients in various suits against me had arrived, wanting to question my former attorneys.

Not only did most people perceive those hated attorneys of mine to be at fault, but in my third-party lawsuits to them, it represented the deep pocket everyone hoped to find. They carried malpractice insurance, after all. At last they were on display, and my vengeful moment of truth had arrived.

As we gathered, I found a quiet corner to myself. It was time for my third prayer. My first had occurred on the road to Lakeland, the second, before my reading the Bible in the motel room in Gainesville, Florida.

I lowered my head and leveled with God. You know how much I hate these attorneys. Without your help, I won't be able to handle it. Unless you calm me I'm afraid I'll jump over the conference table and strangle the no-good—. If what happened in Florida really was you, I need your help. I pray this in the name of Jesus. Amen.

Later at home I knew that—like it or not—Harvey had to hear what happened. I told her what I'd done, how I'd prayed in the name of Jesus, and what had transpired.

"I was cool as a cucumber," I testified in disbelief. "They sat there and lied about one thing after another. Believe it or not, I never got upset, and I even felt compassion. I'm sorry for their families. I don't want them to suffer the way you and Blake have suffered—I mean, the wives and their kids; they haven't done anything to us. It was a miracle. A first-class miracle. I don't see how I could be in the same room with them, listening to the false statements. Suddenly it didn't matter anymore. That was the first miracle. The second happened while they questioned one of those guys. There he was, in the hot seat where I wanted him, trying to answer questions, and he started to cough and choke. Harvey, I got up from that table and brought him a Coke. Can you imagine! I don't know whose compassion that was, but it sure wasn't mine. I don't have one ounce of compassion for those creeps."

Harvey studied me closely, trying to understand, but I couldn't explain what had happened to me. I only knew the stench of the hatred I'd nurtured every day for the last few years; that hatred that motivated almost every thought and action of my life simply evaporated the moment I called upon the name of Jesus.

I didn't understand it at all. I was totally unaware that God was drawing me to himself, step-by-step.

# Chapter 12

# THE BREAKING OF A MAN

At last, things were looking up. My business increased, and I justified taking prime office space within the Omni International Complex in downtown Atlanta. I still gambled, but otherwise, my problems seemed far less formidable.

Anyone would have enjoyed having office space at the Omni, but I had a singular advantage there—that of close proximity to the attorneys I loved to hate. Sometimes I'd be granted a chance run-in with one or the other and could toss off hateful one-liners: "You boys still in business?" "Do you still live in Atlanta?" Or, "Hello, George,* how's tricks?" I found that petty spite could be gratifying. I had read in the paper the previous week that George was one of six people being considered to fill the vacant position of judge of the northern district of Georgia. What pleasure I took in writing each member of the selection panel that George should not be considered a candidate while a suit filed over two years ago claiming legal malpractice was still not settled. I expressed my shock and dismay at George's "lack of full disclosure" to them and that George should now consider withdrawing his name. I knew it would eat George's heart out (and Andy's too, since they were partners), that I would be the one to lecture on lack of full disclosure. I loved it!

A few months later when someone else had been named to the post and I knew George had read the copy of the letter to the selection committee, which I had mailed him of course, I relished our chance meetings. "George, I'm so sorry you didn't get that judgeship. Do you think there was a fly somewhere in the ointment?"

Then, on the morning of May 14, 1978, a telephone call came I shall never forget. I recognized the voice—Gary Eubanks, attorney for numerous individuals who had filed suits against me and my former attorneys. Despite our adversarial positions, I liked and respected Gary. He represented his clients very well.

His voice sounded serious, even urgent. "Steve, I hate to call you so early in the morning with bad news, but I'm sure it's information you need."

I was instantly alert. Gary was not prone to overstatement. "I learned last night that an assistant US attorney is seeking information about you."

"What does that mean?"

"Well, she wouldn't be eliciting information about you unless she planned to take it to the grand jury for the purpose of indicting you."

All the blood seemed to drain from my head. Nausea swept over me, and my body tingled. When I thanked Gary and hung up the phone, I tried to calm myself . . . analyze the situation . . . get a handle on the fear that had taken hold of me.

*What did those people want? There's no way they could know about my recent activities.* Perhaps they had stumbled onto it by some fluke, yet I was confident I had covered my tracks extremely well.

They'd talked to an old investor, so they must have spoken about matters I'd called to the SEC's attention nearly five years before. *Five years! That was it! The five-year statute of limitations on securities violations was nearly up; they must have pulled my file for one last look.*

They could have brought criminal proceedings against me five years ago, had they desired. Why now? What was going to happen to me?

I immediately dialed the phone number of the US attorney's office.

"My name is Stephen Lawson, and I just received information that someone in your office is inquiring about me. I'd like to speak to that person, please."

After a few moments, we were connected. "Mr. Lawson, would you like to make a statement of any kind?"

"No, except that I have nothing to hide and will cooperate with you in every way. Whatever problems I had are past. You know I voluntarily went to the SEC about five years ago."

"Do you have an attorney, Mr. Lawson?"

"I know one I could phone, but I'm not represented at the moment."

"Mr. Lawson, I'd suggest you get one. Good day."

The click of the phone signaled the beginning of worse things to come. I called a friend, who was also the best criminal attorney in Atlanta. Later in the day he called back to say he'd had a lengthy chat with the US attorney's office, and indeed, I had problems. Not current problems, as I'd already figured out, but those old matters I'd disclosed years ago. Now they were intent on seeking an indictment.

At his office, my attorney spelled out the situation in more grim detail. "I'm most concerned because they have your confession on that disclosure document you signed with the SEC five years ago," he said. "It leaves us no defense. Aside from that, your fight now is with the feds. Even if you won, the state securities people could come after you, state by state, because you had investors in so many states. It would be lengthy and costly—a blood bath, even if you won." He went on to say that our best strategy was for me to plead guilty and see if we could work out a deal.

Back at my office, I looked and felt like a walking corpse. I knew I was a finished man. My life was over. Every day for the past five years I'd fought battles real and imagined. But I couldn't fight this.

I dreaded breaking this news to Harvey. "Honey," I told her, sounding as though I was speaking from a bad dream, "it looks as though the SEC isn't through with me."

As I talked through the whole mess with her at home that day, the tears began to flow. For the next several days I couldn't look at Harvey without bursting into tears. I felt unbearable shame about the grief I'd caused my family. I had become everything Mother had said I would.

She said I would fail, and I had failed. I had failed myself and my family far beyond what my mother likely had pictured. As she had always predicted, if I were to approach any kind of success at all, surely I'd push the destruct button and somehow manage to fail. She said I'd end up like Dad. She was right.

In the following days I cried more tears than I thought any person could possess. Harvey and I stopped trying to have conversations because I would break down hopelessly. And she wasn't in much better shape. On May 17 and 18, I had previously planned investor get-togethers in Lexington, Kentucky. Harvey suggested that I keep that appointment since, perhaps, each of us needed to be alone for a while. "We aren't doing much talking anyhow," she pointed out.

I agreed for other reasons. Lexington was as good a place as any to kill myself.

That thought had faintly flickered through my mind at first, but soon I began to believe it presented the best way out—not just for me, but for Harvey and Blake. I realized that kind of legacy was no way for a man to honor his young son, but having your father in jail is no great legacy, either.

If I went to jail, Harvey would surely divorce me and in time marry someone else. That would destroy me. At least with this approach Harvey would acquire considerable life insurance proceeds so she could start her life anew. The two-year incontestability period for suicide (included in all life insurance policies, meaning that no benefits will be paid in the event of suicide until two years after the policy has been issued) had long passed.

Yes, to kill myself would represent for each of us the least of all the evils. As long as Harvey would remarry anyway, at least she could have enough money to prevent her from marrying someone else just for the sake of his providing for them.

Blake wouldn't remember me when he grew up. I could imagine him telling people close to him, "I don't remember my real father at all. He committed suicide when I was four. Mom remarried, and as far as I'm concerned, *he's* always been a dad to me."

Darkness engulfed me. Satan, disguising my pride, ego, and selfishness as honor, integrity, and responsibility, lured me closer and closer to the edge of self-destruction.

These morbid thoughts were heightened by my absolute refusal to endure public scorn a second time or to go to prison. No, I couldn't do it. Dead men are never indicted. My decision was the only possible decision, and I'd enact it quickly.

In Lexington, the night before my scheduled meetings, I perfected my plans. One of my investors owned a sporting goods store, and I'd buy a gun there first thing in the morning. Sleep didn't come. I was imprisoned in my hotel room, waiting through one of those nights that took forever to turn into dawn. I tossed, turned, and sobbed. I had to do something. If I'd had a gun, it would have been the right time.

I considered phoning Harvey, but I had nothing to say, and it was silly to wake her in the event she was able to sleep. The note I'd leave would say it all, anyhow. *Oh, how I loved her. Would she ever forgive me? Could she go through the rest of her life without hating me? Dear God, what had I done to her?*

The clock read 3:00 a.m. It would be six or seven hours before I could buy the gun. Things I'd read and thought about—books Don Patterson had left in my mailbox, arguments about Jesus and the Bible, and prayers—all flooded into my consciousness. Turning over a new leaf wasn't what was needed—a new life was. Not merely repentance but regeneration. I dropped to my knees before the sofa and rested my elbows on the seat, with my head buried in my hands. I began to speak through my sobs.

"Dear God, I can't do it anymore. I have no fight left, and I'm going to kill myself. . . . I know that Jesus was your Son; I've read enough to believe that. You know how much I loved Dad, how I don't want to desecrate his memory, but I don't think this does. If anything would, it's the shame I've brought to his name through all these things I've done.

"Lord, I've had a life of successes and failures like anyone else. But now I'm at the end of my rope. Please hear my prayer, come into my heart, and make me a new person. I have nothing to give you, but please take me anyway. I want to be a Christian. Thank you, Father. It's *in the name of Jesus* that I pray."

I didn't feel better immediately. The hotel room still felt like a prison, containing one desperate, exhausted inmate. Only later would I realize that the continual sobbing had dwindled to intermittent tears. Also, I'd forgotten all about the sporting goods store. I returned home to Harvey.

At home, my general mood was one of frustration and anger. For a long time I'd admired the Pattersons, their character and their lifestyle, yet I'd invited Jesus into my life, and nothing had happened. I didn't feel one bit different.

I asked Harvey to phone the Pattersons and tell them we had to see them—tonight. I told Harvey that I had prayed to become a Christian. That blockbuster didn't produce the hostile response I'd expected. *Perhaps she just hurt too much…or maybe she was just walking through the final stages of our marriage and life together.*

She didn't have the old fight, either. She appeared to be calm, but I guessed it was controlled hysteria. I couldn't blame her. When Patti and Don greeted us at the door they could tell that we weren't there for small talk. We were quickly ushered to a table beside their swimming pool, and Patti brought glasses of lemonade from the pool house. We talked, but Harvey remained quiet.

I could see that she was as numb as I was and that she was present only because I had insisted. Out of love for me she was willing to try anything. At that point I was sure our marriage would not survive all this, and Harvey was doing the things that would allow her to look back someday and say she'd done everything she could.

The Pattersons listened intently as I told all about my life and the events of the past several days. I wept the entire time. At last I concluded my tirade, saying, "I asked Jesus to come into my life, and I don't feel any different. What did I do wrong? Is there a spiritual protocol I don't know about?"

For the first time, I was asking Don questions he couldn't answer, and that upset me.

"I know God chooses us and not the other way around," I continued. "Could it be that I want him, but he doesn't want me?"

I had experienced the rejection of friends and before that the condemnation of my own mother. Apparently I could surmount those things, but knowledge, borne on a tide of deep grief, made me think that God's rejection would be the final, unbearable indictment.

Don and Patti answered unhesitatingly that could not be a possibility. Then Patti turned to Harvey. "Harvey, how do you feel about what Steve has done? What's *your* reaction?"

It was the first time Harvey had been invited to speak. She'd sat there all this time, watching the way one might if caught at an intersection where two cars sped full throttle toward one another.

"Fine, I guess," she said. "I asked Jesus into my life too, the other night."

I stared at her in disbelief. *Harvey?* I might have been an unlikely candidate for knowing the Lord, but Harvey was even more so.

Patti and Don brightened up at that. "Tell us about it!" Patti said.

"My feelings have been much the same as Stephen's. Last night while he was in Lexington, I couldn't sleep. At three in the morning I was wide awake and lying there scared, contemplating the future. I was soaked with perspiration, so I got up to take a shower. I bowed my head so the water could hit the back of my neck and suddenly found myself on my knees. That's when I asked Jesus to come into my life. . . . Apparently Stephen and I did it within fifteen minutes of each other."

"And how do *you* feel, Harvey?" asked Patti.

"Pretty much the same as he does. Nothing much."

Soon we left, taking our frustrations with us. As we pulled out of the Pattersons' driveway, I told Harvey angrily, "Whatever it was I expected to find by coming here tonight, I sure didn't get it. This whole thing must be a bunch of garbage. There may be a God, and Jesus may be his Son, but they're surely not interested in me."

The next morning Harvey and I arose at our usual time. Something felt different. Something *was* different. Though we each realized it, we tried to analyze the feeling before being bold enough to share it with the other.

At last, Harvey spoke. "Honey, we weathered the other deal, and we'll weather this one too. Let's face it together."

Those were the first positive words either of us had uttered in days. As we continued to speak, we realized what had happened—God had infused us with the Holy Spirit. Our sadness had begun to turn into joy. The bitterness turned into love, and the trauma, into peace. Defeat became hope. We had been given his free gift of faith, filled to the brim and overflowing. I had begun to forgive, and I felt completely forgiven by God and by Harvey.

Now there was reason not only to live but to rejoice. For the next three months Harvey and I stayed on a "high" from which it seemed we'd never descend. One day, as we left a department store, Harvey said she'd just met an old friend, who told her she looked wonderful.

"You know, I should have said, 'Why shouldn't I look good? My husband is going to the slammer, and we're broke,' " Harvey joked, her blue eyes dancing. Then she was suddenly wistful. "Do you think we'll go through life like this—so happy?"

I knew exactly what she meant. "Why didn't we accept Jesus years ago?" The truth was clear: *I had been in prison all my life, and now I was free.*

I read the Bible voraciously. Each page seemed to have been written especially to me. My prayer life was beyond any description I could give it. I didn't pray for needs as much as having the desire and joy of being in conversation with God.

# Chapter 13

# GRACE PERIOD

The Sunday following our conversation with the Pattersons, the leader of the adult Sunday school class at the Episcopal Cathedral of St. Philip asked if anyone had something to share. Like a shot, I stood and told everyone what had happened to Harvey and me. This was our first time in years to attend church other than for a holiday or a baptism. We were visitors in this class. But the newfound life and joy overcame any shyness I might have had otherwise.

I admitted I was Jewish and confessed that I'd hidden that fact in the past but told everyone I was proud to be a completed Jew. Now I understood that Jews had not only been given a birthright but also the power to choose. There was a difference between Jews as they had evolved in their religious history and how the Lord had intended them to be. I told them that I chose to be chosen—chosen to be an heir with Christ. It was the first of many such testimonies I'd give in the months to come.

Harvey and I received a tremendous hunger for the Word of God. We were enthusiastic about opportunities for Bible study, prayer groups, teaching ministries, and occasions to witness. It was a great experience to share as a couple our first adventures with God.

Meanwhile, my attorney and I continued to grapple with my problems with the US attorney's office. I tried to find ways to earn money to provide for Harvey and Blake should I go to prison, but nothing turned up. At the same time, I was compiling a long list of those persons I knew I had wronged and to whom I must go to ask their forgiveness. Those visits were never easy, yet each time I did what Jesus commanded, I was blessed far more than I could have expected.

Don Patterson suggested that I write to my former attorneys and ask for their forgiveness. I resisted; those years of intense, unrelenting, murderous hatred were hard to relinquish. But I knew Don was right. How could I not forgive, when I had been forgiven so much? But it was more than that. Even though these two men weren't Christians, the Lord had used them in such a powerful way to bring me to the end of myself. Was there any way to tell them that overnight my feelings of hatred had turned to love and that they were constantly in my prayers? I agreed to compose the letter and read it to Don before mailing it.

In truth, I could apologize to those attorneys and former enemies for many of my actions, but there were things, in good conscience, for which I could not apologize. Wrestle though I might, I knew the key was forgiveness. The moment I dropped the letters in the mailbox a tremendous weight lifted off my heart. And I wept there—right on the street corner.

Later, George's and Andy's comments were passed back to me regarding my letters to them: "Tom* is a great criminal attorney and knows what he's doing. Lawson is capable of anything at this point, but this religious copout is a defense I wouldn't have figured him for." They remained convinced that I fully deserved to go to prison.

My new attorney, an old friend, was frank with me. "Steve, I shouldn't be saying this and don't intend to elaborate, but you wouldn't be going through all this if you hadn't gone for those two guys' jugular veins. For a number of years you have acted on the basest sort of emotions; they haven't. They understand the law and how the system works. You thought you were sticking it to them when all the time they were beating you to death."

As these various events transpired, Harvey and I began to know and love one another in a whole new dimension, that of the Spirit of God. The love we'd always had for one another paled in comparison to this new love we shared together in Christ. There came a fresh intimacy, great and precious, a bond that only Christian husbands and wives can understand.

We marveled at being captured by Christ—separately but on the same day, even the same hour! As Harvey described it, "I didn't come to the Lord because of Stephen's problems. His issues only made clear to me that I had my own conflicts, turmoil, and flaws. I had become as desperate as he and was without any peace. We had always been best friends and were a fortress of strength unto ourselves up until these disastrous events. When we lost our money, for the most part, we lost our friends. We vowed to be kind to one another in spite of everything, but our lives were unraveling.

"Blake, the joy of our lives, was two months old when Stephen's house of cards began to collapse. Blake was only fourteen months old when I had to return to work, which I have always regretted.

"As time went on, Stephen and I talked about nothing but litigation—what might happen, our chances of being restored. The hatred boiling in Stephen affected me deeply. His poison fed me too. I had begun to develop a hard edge. I saw Blake's babyhood slipping away, my husband was involved in one horrible problem after another, and loneliness almost destroyed me.

"I began to jog each night, hoping to dissolve some of my tension and desperate unhappiness. As I ran, I tried to clear my head. I'd talk to God, a God I doubted was there. I told him how much Stephen's problems frightened me and that I needed help. How I wished there was someone with whom I could converse about ordinary things, not realizing until later that is a part of prayer and talking with our Father in heaven.

"Oh, I was so scared and vulnerable, scared of losing Stephen as well as losing my own soul. I didn't think God was listening. I had become cynical. One night I told him, "If you are God, prove that I can run a mile without stopping." I felt an invisible hand in the middle of my back, pushing. I ran that mile and kept on going.

"That's the way it was until that night in the shower. The morning after our visit with the Pattersons, we both entered into perfect peace. Christ entered our lives in such a dramatic fashion and changed our entire perspective on how to live and to love each other. My confidant and best friend was and is Stephen with Christ in the center of our lives."

Harvey and I were given the sacrament of water baptism by an ordained minister in the Pattersons' swimming pool, and they presented me with a new Bible—one that is held together today by rubber bands because it's had so much use.

Three weeks after I became a Christian, I attended a prayer group where a person mentioned something called the "baptism in the Holy Spirit."

"If there is something *more*," I blurted, "I want it!" The next day several Christian brothers met with me and prayed me through deliverance, inner healing, and the empowering from God's Spirit. I was freed that day from a lot of the sludge of my past life.

Two weeks later, Harvey was freed in the same way. We didn't see then the importance of God's timing. He was preparing us, strengthening us, and setting our feet on a firm place. Soon would come trials that the old Steve and Harvey could not have endured.

Those first seven months following my conversion, I lived in a kind of euphoria. Both Harvey and I saw the world through fresh eyes. We were filled with joy and gratitude. At last I had accepted myself—my failures, problems, and sins—because I had accepted Christ to be the guide of my life. And I was even more interested in learning about the God who had freed me, since he was also the God of my Jewish heritage.

For the first time, my life had a transparency—no more clouded words, disguises, ambiguous and deceptive meanings. Since I wasn't afraid of who I was, I could be myself.

More and more, I was given opportunities to give my Christian testimony. At those times, Satan would attack. I'd feel such pain in my knees and ankles that on many occasions I'd have to drag myself to the car. By the time I spoke, however, the pain would be gone. There are two things the Evil One detests: first, for a person to become a Christian; and second, for that person to become an effective Christian. One evening Harvey and I had decided to see a movie—not a frequent event for us. We were primed for a light, fun-filled evening. Armed with popcorn and Cokes, we settled back to enjoy a very funny film. And the movie was living up to our expectations except that after the first half hour, I didn't see it.

Suddenly, I was alone with Satan. It was like being in an isolation booth. I heard no sounds, and though I watched the screen, I didn't comprehend what I saw. All I knew was that I had to kill myself.

There was no logical thought process to this as there had been when I was back in Lexington, months ago. I simply felt an overpowering compunction to kill myself *right now.*

I couldn't utter a sound. My entire attention focused on getting it done. *How? Where?* Had there been a gun in my car, I'm sure I would have left the theater right then and killed myself in the parking lot. Prayer was beyond my grasp.

Somehow, I started breathing the name of Jesus—"Jesus, Jesus, Jesus"—over and over again. The war seemed to go on forever. The movie ended, I saw the lights come on, and Harvey and I moved from the theater amidst a stream of other people. Outside, in hurried expressions of distress, I turned to her and blurted out what was happening to me.

We sat in the car and prayed, talked, then prayed some more. We left the parking lot, stopped at a gas station for a fill-up, and ended up in a restaurant, where we talked for hours.

From the time we entered the restaurant, the ominous feelings were gone; in fact, I'd never felt better. But that experience drove home a point for me and gave some insight to a question that I often hear: "Can a person who is a Christian commit suicide?" The devil is real and will pound at our weaknesses. That night could have turned out differently. It strengthens me to know that Jesus came to destroy the works of the devil (1 John 3:8).

As the storm clouds of my life moved in rapidly during 1978, I realized that my conversion to Christ was for me and me alone. The condemnation from other Jews was more than I can easily express. Moreover, even Christians had suspicions about the veracity of someone who might be grasping at straws "in the name of the Lord" because he appeared to be on his way to jail. For the first time, I consciously decided to place my eyes on God and on how *God* saw me rather than worry about what people might think. And for the first time, appearance and impressions cut no ice whatsoever. It was just the new me out there for people to see and judge as they would. I was out of the impressions business—no more slick talk and put-on personality.

Later I would discover that my commitment made me a partner with Jesus, and I would discover union with him. I would find him to be all I needed and desired. He would prove himself faithful, sufficient, forgiving, merciful, and just. I knew, without a doubt, that my salvation was proof that the gospel is valid in modern-day life.

And later I would more fully understand that I had been forgiven completely and that I was truly reconciled to my heavenly Father. He was equipping me, through Jesus, to be the man who, on my own, I had no power, ability, or authority to be.

It didn't happen at once—that understanding. It took time to firmly establish the facts in a mind and heart that had been conditioned to believe and see in other ways. Jesus really did take my place when he died on Calvary. Satan had been beaten. After a time, even that enemy could not convince me that my sins still stood in the way; I was certain, heart and soul, that all my wrongs had been cancelled by God.

I had been through a breaking period, when everything had fallen apart. I had been hopeless; now I experienced the power of God's grace, grounded in the knowledge provided in the previous years of reading and study. I had called out to the Lord, and he heard—and delivered me from my fears.

# Chapter 14

# WITHOUT ONE PLEA

Tim and Alice invited us for lunch at the Commerce Club. They were to stand with Harvey and me at the time of my sentencing, and Tim wanted to say a few words on my behalf to the judge.

These were close, comfortable friends with whom we had always shared New Year's Eve. Both Harvey and Alice are exceptional cooks, and we'd feasted on many gourmet dinners at our house or theirs. Once we had vacationed together in Bermuda.

Tim and Alice stuck with us when my business went under in 1974, when I couldn't pay the rent, and when there were no funds for insurance payments. They stood by when I entered my consent order with the SEC and when I learned I would be indicted. Still they were our friends, sharing a special lunch and a monumental concern over one more tough event—my sentencing.

After I became a Christian, I was eager to bring all the dark deeds to light. At one point, my attorney had said that I actually might win this case in court. He would have to depend on the US attorney's over trying her case, which he felt she was likely to do.

The problem with that, I explained, was that I was guilty as charged. I wanted to embark on my new life in Christ with old things truly past. That meant I must even admit to things the court knew nothing about and would depend on God to watch over me as I revealed the truth.

For years I had fought one battle after another—with the SEC, my former attorneys, old investors—and I had no desire to fight another. My attorney promised to do the very best he could and advised me not to worry about the expense. He knew I had no money; he agreed to receive payment at some future time.

I wish I could relate that it was easy to plead guilty, but it was not. The government originally was willing to accept my pleading guilty to two counts. Now, with new information, the government insisted on raising the ante. I would plead guilty to three counts. It took nearly ten months to agree on the litany of those crimes that, in good conscience, I could plead. Discussion after discussion took place in the US attorney's offices. I gave the assistant US attorney private seminars on real estate so she could have the general background necessary to understand how my crimes were committed, of what I was clearly guilty, and of what I was clearly innocent. At last we agreed, and I signed the plea admitting my guilt.

Thus I had drawn a line that separated the new Stephen Lawson from the old. The old Stephen had been another person. Many months later, in a news magazine, I came across a statement from former president Richard Nixon that delineates so well my former thinking and actions.

What starts the process, really, are laughs and slights and snubs when you are a kid . . . if your anger is deep enough and strong enough, you learn that you can change those attitudes by excellence, personal gut performance. . . . It's a piece of cake until you get to the top. You find you can't stop playing the game the way you've always played it. . . . So you are lean and mean and resourceful and you continue to walk on the edge of the precipice because over the years you have become fascinated by how close to the edge you can walk without losing your balance.

As the four of us walked toward the court house, there was little conversation but many silent prayers. I thought, Steve, if you could change all this in one second's time—return to 1973 and have things the way they were and not know the Lord—or be here now, perhaps on the way to prison but knowing the Lord, which would you choose?

I would go to prison gladly if that were a prerequisite for my knowing the Lord. I broke the silence to tell Harvey my thoughts, and she squeezed my hand in agreement.

We recognized several faces as we approached the courtroom. There were people from the state and federal securities departments and a man from the postal department. The assistant US attorney brought her boss. I recalled seeing my name on the indictment: UNITED STATES OF AMERICA vs. STEPHEN P. LAWSON. It appeared that the United States of America was well represented.

Judge Warner* was presiding, a good sign, my attorney thought, in that he was considered one of the more compassionate judges in Atlanta. When my name was called, my attorney asked if people could speak on my behalf, and the judge nodded his permission.

Tim Jones spoke, testifying to our long friendship and the dramatic change in me since I had become a Christian and asking the judge to be merciful in his decision.

Then Harvey spoke at length, explaining her love for me and at the same time her frustration over what my actions had done to our lives. "I'm the mother of a beautiful five-year-old, and we don't deserve what has happened to us. We have been publicly ridiculed and have lost all our money. I don't know what Stephen's fate might be, but I know I could leave him and try to make a new life for myself." She went on to explain her own conversion to faith in Christ, that both of us were new people, and she had forgiven me for what I had done. She believed I was worthy of her confidence—and the judge's.

After she finished, I spoke for myself for a few minutes. Then my attorney added these words: "Your Honor, Stephen and his wife have been friends of my wife and me for many years. He just got caught up in trying to be successful because he envied some of his friends who lived on the northwest side of town."

I could hardly believe my ears. Whose side was he on, anyway? He continued in this vein, and then the assistant US attorney spoke, presenting the US government's side quite thoroughly. When she finished we waited for the verdict. Tom had speculated that if I had to serve time it wouldn't exceed six months. Although I hoped for the best, in my heart I knew the roof was about to cave in. For, in truth, had I been the judge and heard what had been presented, I would have given a long, tough sentence.

Without emotion, Judge Warner looked me in the eye and said he was sentencing me to four years on one count of mail fraud and four years on one count of security violations, the time to run consecutively. On the third count he sentenced me to five years of probation, to begin after my prison sentence had been served.

Eight years of confinement! I was so stunned I had to ask my attorney if I had heard correctly. I wasn't the only one taken by surprise; the judge was about to leave the bench when Tom regained the presence of mind to ask the judge to allow me to turn myself in to whatever facility was to be designated and to allow me forty-five days to get my affairs into order. This was granted.

There was a brief booking downstairs where fingerprints and mug shots were taken, and within half an hour, I was free to leave. We shook hands with my attorney and departed, the Lawsons and Joneses, still in shock.

Several weeks later I learned that I would go to Eglin Federal Prison Camp in Fort Walton Beach, Florida. Just months before, a law had been changed, affecting where I could be sent. Previously, anyone with a sentence of five years or longer could not qualify for an "honor camp" but had to do his time in a maximum-security "gladiator" camp such as the Atlanta penitentiary.

Harvey started looking for a job. She needed a good one that would provide a greater salary than any she'd had in the past. Within a few days, she received a job offer with exactly the salary for which we'd been praying. She could start right away, while I was at home, and I could help out while she eased into her new routine.

We worked out a household budget, stripping expenses to cover only the most necessary items. Her new salary would not quite stretch; she would need another $300 dollars per month.

"That's not too bad, though," I commented. "I'm sure that some of our brothers and sisters in Christ will gladly donate some money each month to your well-being if I ask." I made a prospective list. If six people gave fifty dollars a month, that would do it.

When the first several people looked me in the eye and said no, I wasn't discouraged. But the list continued and one no followed another.

"Don't feel bad for having asked. I'd do the same thing," one man told me.

"Why don't you sell some of your furniture?" another suggested.

"Why can't Harvey move to a cheaper apartment?" someone else said.

Finally, a brother suffering a sudden attack of wisdom offered the coup de grâce: "The Lord has told me to tell you that Harvey must live on her salary and make whatever sacrifices she must to be self-sufficient." In donating his opinion he had named Jesus as an innocent accomplice.

*Could this be happening?* I was shocked to learn that Christians didn't have the closeness that Jewish people exhibit toward one another at times like these. I hurt badly, not only for my family, but for those in our Christian family who had said no.

At length I decided to visit Grace Kinser, a dear and wise friend of sixty-plus years who was such an encourager in the faith to Harvey and me. I filled her in on what I'd tried to accomplish in Harvey's behalf. "Grace, can it be that all these people are speaking God's will?" I asked. "Can it be that he wants my family to suffer because I was out of his will? Doesn't he care what will happen to my family?"

I looked up and saw that she was in tears.

"Steve, let's pray for them and forgive them for their actions," she said, softly. After a moment of prayer, she asked for a list of those I'd visited. Very, very reluctantly I gave it to her.

A few days after I left for prison, our friends, including those on my list, arrived at Grace's home for fellowship and refreshments. Then Grace rose and told everyone why she had asked them to meet. She opened her Bible, read several passages, shared her perceptions of Scripture and our family, and then asked how much each would give as a monthly love offering. By evening's end an individual had been appointed to receive the funds and for the next several months present a check to Harvey.

This group was augmented by others from the Cathedral of St. Philip who felt it was God's will that they share our financial burden. Only three weeks after my arrival at prison, our friend Bob phoned Harvey. "At this morning's prayer breakfast, we asked for pledges of support and received pledges and checks for more than $4,000. People have called my office all day, and the amount has risen to more than $7,000!"

These heartfelt, anonymous gifts gave continual, tangible proof of the love, grace and mercy of God in people's hearts. Their effect on us rose far beyond any dollars-and-cents total.

Thus I learned some vitally important lessons. I learned that I must look ultimately to God because people will let you down (at least in their initial, human responses). And I must trust God to be the one to provide for my family.

Many times during those weeks before prison, I was asked to witness for Christ. Each of these occasions strengthened me immeasurably. I shall always remember my final evening before departing for prison. I had been invited by Gary Eubanks to speak at the First Baptist Church of Marietta. Gary was the attorney who had represented some twenty of my former clients to whom I now owed more than $200,000. He and I were still legal adversaries. But we also were brothers in Christ, and he was bold enough to invite me to speak at his church.

I closed my testimony that night explaining that I was standing on 1 Peter 5:5–10:

In the same way, you who are younger, submit yourselves to your elders. All of you, clothe yourselves with humility toward one another, because, "God opposes the proud but shows favor to the humble." Humble yourselves, therefore, under God's mighty hand, that he may lift you up in due time. Cast all your anxiety on him because he cares for you.

Be alert and of sober mind. Your enemy the devil prowls around like a roaring lion looking for someone to devour. Resist him, standing firm in the faith, because you know that the family of believers throughout the world is undergoing the same kind of sufferings.

And the God of all grace, who called you to his eternal glory in Christ, after you have suffered a little while, will himself restore you and make you strong, firm and steadfast.

*Chapter 15*

# FAMILY VISIT

"It is nonsense to say God fills the gap," Dietrich Bonhoeffer wrote. "He does not fill it, but keeps it empty so that our communion with another may be kept alive, even at the cost of pain. The dearer and richer our memories, the more difficult the separation. From the moment we awake until we fall asleep we must commend our loved ones wholly and unreservedly to God, and leave them in his hands, transforming our anxiety for them into prayers on their behalf."

I had been at Eglin for two weeks and understood the experiences and attitudes that shaped Bonhoeffer's words. Each morning before I arose, I'd pray for Harvey's and Blake's well-being. At times I wondered if I had really turned them over to God or if I cared about them as much as I should. Although I felt peaceful, *was I really at peace or had my love and caring turned to indifference? Had the miles between us made more of a difference than I cared to admit? Had I become so concerned about myself and my prison life that I felt too little concern for them?*

All my life caring had meant doing, or at least worrying. But now, unable to do anything, I felt a strange peace; it transcended anything I could conjure up. Further, the more I relied on God, the more he seemed to provide. I began to learn that I couldn't rely on my feelings. I had to concentrate on trusting a God outside of myself and beyond my own powerlessness. And I had to wait and see how life would unfold.

Friday came. Harvey and Blake were driving down from Atlanta and would stay with the Culps that weekend. They'd arrive in Destin early that evening and would meet me in the prison visiting room at nine the next morning.

Though Harvey and I had been married thirteen years, I'd been through several stages of acquiring a new crush on her. I never grew tired of her expressive face and her equally engaging conversation. There was still something about watching her walk into a room that made my heart pound.

Anticipating Harvey's arrival was almost more than I could stand. I acted a lot like a kid on his first date. I got up at the crack of dawn, shaving around my newly acquired beard and getting ready to see her. In my mind, the day had nearly passed by the time I saw their car approaching.

I worried for a moment. How did I look dressed in my prison outfit, beginning to grow the beard I'd always wanted? What kind of atmosphere would the visiting area offer Blake? Would he be ashamed of me? Perhaps I should have been clean-shaven so my appearance would be the same.

"Stephen Lawson, 07209, you have a visitor," bellowed a voice from the loud speaker. I hurried to the visiting area to meet them. Harvey and Blake each did a double take as

I walked through the door. The beard, my prison garb, and the loss of about ten pounds somewhat took them aback.

"Daddy!" Blake yelled, running toward me after a tiny hesitation. I picked him up and gave him a long, long hug. Harvey and I embraced.

She had brought a basket full of goodies from home, and we found a table outside and proceeded to unpack her feast. She had even baked brioche for me, a fancy party roll that I particularly liked.

Harvey and I wanted and needed to discuss so many things but could accomplish only a portion of what we'd hoped as Blake kept running over from the swing area to demand my attention.

It was wonderful, being with Harvey. I could actually lean over and touch her arm. And to hear her reassuring words—that made life worth living, worth getting through my time in this place.

Blake reacted well to this new environment. The place didn't look like a jail. There were no people with guns, no guard towers, bars, or high walls. It matched the description I'd given him the morning I left home: a place where daddies go when they've made mistakes. Indeed, other daddies were there that morning and also many children Blake's age.

It was exhilarating to be a family again, even under our circumstances and for the short time involved. Harvey and I felt God's presence in our daily happenings and efforts, despite our separation. Watching Blake as he played with another inmate's child in the prison yard, we were amazed at how we could experience such normalcy in this difficult atmosphere.

Prior to my leaving, Blake had been accepted into one of Atlanta's excellent private schools. Yet, after my sentencing, we knew that tuition expenses were out of the question. So I was dumbfounded to learn from Harvey that Blake's tuition would be paid by parents of one of his preschool classmates, also accepted at the school, until my return.

"You're joking!" I exclaimed. Who on earth would do such a generous thing? When Harvey told me, I was mystified. I'd never even heard of the people. Harvey had other news, equally moving. Her mother had helped us with carpools and the myriad other jobs that go with assisting a busy working mother and an active small boy. Renee, Harvey's sister, went even further. She leased her furnished home in order to move in with Harvey and help with everything from rent to keeping house. Two magnificent ladies— just like Harvey. I was overwhelmed.

Blake climbed onto my lap. He seemed much heavier than the last time I'd held him. "Daddy?"

"What, honey?"

"When you came to prison, why did you take all the money with you?"

The innocent question flashed like a bolt of lightning. It was two weeks into the ordeal, and already he was noticing the economic difference. Not only that, he assumed that I was taking the money, rather than realizing that we simply didn't have any.

Harvey and I attempted to explain. It wasn't what we said that helped, I think, but rather that Blake saw his father and mother united on the subject. After our explanation, he smiled. "Okay," he said. "But after you get out of here, will you go to work and help Mommy earn some money? She's working really hard."

Such remarks are a man's real punishment; they go far beyond the judge's intent at the time of sentencing.

Saturday and Sunday sped by. I walked Blake and Harvey to the door and watched as she made several trips to the car, carrying articles from the visiting area. Aside from the picnic hamper and food items that Harvey carried, she also brought Blake's first two-wheeler bike so that I could see he had learned to ride it just since I had left home. I was not allowed to assist her and hated watching her struggle with heavy items.

When time came to say good-bye, Blake began to cry and begged to stay. I held him for ten minutes, talking to him as I carried him around the visiting area. For each of us, the good-bye was difficult. For days after, I felt horrible.

"The first visit's always the hardest," advised a fellow inmate. "Take my word for it, it gets easier. And always remember: the visit's not for you, but for your family. Make sure your spirits are high, so your positive attitude will reinforce theirs." I took that as a direct message from the Lord and tucked it into my heart.

From Harvey's perspective, the visit was far from over:

As we drove away, I talked calmly to Blake, but inside I panicked. I hadn't thought he would cry so; I hadn't thought I would be so devastated myself. We had been so "up" for the trip, so excited about seeing Stephen. But I wasn't prepared for such a letdown.

"Wasn't it wonderful visiting with Daddy?" I asked Blake.

"Yes, but why can't he come home with us?"

"Daddy will be home someday—soon, I hope—and it will be great to be a family again. Didn't Daddy look different with his beard? Did it tickle when he kissed you?"

Blake started to cry again, and when I couldn't console him with words, I pulled the car off the road and cuddled him for a few moments. I prayed and asked God to give us the strength to drive the 350 miles back to Atlanta. I asked for peace for both Blake and me and courage to make it through the next week.

This was my life now, that of a single parent. It was hard. But it was okay. God was continually faithful to Blake and me. I remembered the last drive like this when it was just Liz and me, after leaving Stephen two weeks before. I had asked the Lord to help me through the next several days. *Had it been that long already?* We had made it through the first two weeks. The visit with Stephen had been so natural. Maybe, just maybe, Blake and I could make it, after all.

Chapter 16

# INVISIBLE SUPPORT

On "the outside," I'd attended many prayer group meetings. Yet none could compare with those that met at 4:30 p.m. each day at Eglin.

We were prisoners. We had acute, obvious needs to confess and pray about. Unlike those groups at home, ours included men with various backgrounds of education, race, culture, and denomination. Our group changed constantly as some members got released and new members arrived.

At Eglin, as at other prisons, everyone looked the same and no facades are erected to say, "I'm okay." Former politicians, heads of large corporations, and civic leaders mingled their lives with dope pushers and armed robbers. Dressed in hand-me-down Air Force blues and without access to blow-dryers for our hair, my fellow inmates and I looked equally undistinguished and disreputable.

From this group of people, however, emerged several who loved God enough to serve the others, thus assuming some degree of spiritual leadership. Chaplain George Castillo, who headed all religious programs at Eglin, served as our official leader.

Chaplain Castillo was perhaps the hardest working and least appreciated man—by the staff, at least—at Eglin. None of us could fail to appreciate his gracious spirit in that no-win job, caught as he was between inmates and administration.

He had to program a full range of services—Roman Catholic, Protestant, Spanish Mass, *Jumu'ah* prayers—and even make time for the Black Awareness Choir to rehearse. Then there was the Chapel Choir, the responsibility for driving Jewish inmates to services held on the Air Force base, plus the Bible study programs scheduled in the evenings when people from the First Baptist Church of Fort Walton Beach would come in to teach.

Our prayer group learned about faith in action. As prisoners we soon learned we could change very little about our lives. We were told when to eat, sleep, and work. Before prison, if my wife phoned to say the air conditioning system wasn't working or we needed a major plumbing repair, I'd take care of it. In prison we could do almost nothing about what happened at home—except pray. In that stark setting, I learned much about effective prayer.

We prayed for one another. Some men entered the group in the lowest of emotional states. For them, the Lord provided special strength and encouragement. Others had not yet recognized their need for Jesus because they had never faced up to their own desperation. Although impregnated with disillusionment, they came to meet God. We learned that Jesus could and would meet us at our point of need.

We kept a simple format: thirty minutes devoted to conversation and listing prayer requests followed by thirty minutes of prayer. Our talk wasn't always spiritual; often it centered on secular events and our personal frustrations. Sometimes I attended out of duty more than anything else.

Despite our emotional and spiritual limitations, we began to love one another. A bond developed among us; we became soul mates. It's impossible to live with people— to share their spiritual peaks and valleys, their intimate dreams, and fervently pray for them in the group and individually—without growing very close. We came to know one another's families because we prayed for them so often. "How's Jane's back doing?" we'd ask, as though we were well acquainted with Jane, although we had never met her. Our prayer group at first numbered three or four, but ultimately included as many as forty. At first I assumed everyone had pretty much the same sort of spiritual experiences as I'd had, but that wasn't the case.

A person comes in contact with real characters in such a setting, people who would look unbelievable in any other place. Such a person was Joe "The Butcher."

Joe had served about eight years at the Atlanta penitentiary before coming to Eglin. That in itself is rather unusual because the Atlanta pen is where the most hard-core criminals are warehoused. People at the Atlanta pen *never* left because a guy with a twenty-year stint was considered a short timer. Not only that, the Atlanta pen was a maximum-security prison, whereas Eglin was far from that. If you wanted to escape from Eglin all you had to do was call a cab and sneak over the white line that was painted on the cement to indicate the point over which inmates were not allowed to pass. Many people have said that a place like Eglin is a much tougher place to do time than at one of the real joints, as they are called. Being almost free is very hard on a man, where if you are really "locked down," it is easier to come to grips with your situation.

Joe had been one of the short timers at the Atlanta pen, as he had only a sixteen-year sentence. What he did and what he actually got caught doing isn't my story to relate. The truth is that The Butcher often said he wished he was able to give his complete story and witness to God's work in his life but that some of the things he had been involved with had no statute of limitations. So I never pressed, and he never offered more than a few snatches. Reportedly, he was a Mafia chieftain. He certainly looked the part; at fifty-three years of age he was about five feet five and weighed about 230 pounds of solid muscle. He used to bench press 450 pounds but claimed that, since he was older and the sun was so hot in the middle of summer, he had "tapered down to just 375."

I vividly remember Joe's first couple of days at Eglin. He is the type of guy who has never met a stranger. Aside from that, I'm fairly confident that his arrival was known and quietly publicized, because as soon as he set foot on the compound, every Italian was there to welcome him. It was something you had to see to believe. Anywhere he walked he was followed by as many as ten to twenty inmates. If he said hello to a person, *everyone* said hello in return. If he told a joke, everyone laughed. And other people's jokes were considered funny only if The Butcher laughed at them.

One of those first days, The Butcher and his armada came sailing down the sidewalk. I said hello and nodded but received no response. (I later found out he was practically blind without glasses and merely hadn't seen me.) Another day the group passed me again, and I ventured to say, "How's it going?" The Butcher stared at me and said, "Okay, okay." I was so amazed that this big shot had spoken to me that I responded, kindly, of course, "Well, praise God."

At that point The Butcher stopped in his tracks and wheeled around, a big grin on his face. "Yeah, yeah, praise the Lord, brother. You know the Lord? Yeah? Good! Nice to meet you, brother, What's your name? Steve Lawson, huh? I'll try to remember, but I'm not too good with names, you know what I mean?"

All this time, he was shaking my hand, and the pain from his grip shot almost up to my armpit.

"Listen, Lawson, you come to The Butcher's cube. We'll talk some. I got some fruit in. You like peaches?"

With that, the group continued on their way, but I noticed that they smiled to me and let me know that I had passed some kind of test. That evening I looked up The Butcher in his cube. After all, he had extended an invitation, and it certainly wouldn't be wise to run the risk of offending or insulting him.

As I approached his cube, it appeared as though "Little Italy" was having a block party. In the middle of all the people, The Butcher was holding court. When our eyes met, he sprang into action. "Okay, youse guys, clear out. I got company. Come in, come in."

He asked me my name again, and I invited him to call me Steve.

"The name's Joe 'The Butcher.' Call me anything you like. Most people just call me Joe or refer to me as 'The Butcher.' Take a peach for yourself. They're in my locker."

"No, thanks. I'm not hungry."

"I said, 'Take a peach,' " The Butcher stated. "What do I have to do—break your arm?"

"As a matter of fact, I'd love a peach," I replied.

We settled back and talked. There was an unmistakable charm about this hulk of a man, and when you looked into his eyes or when he grinned, Jesus was all over his face. We were to see each other daily at prayer group. However, I would be tested for several months before being totally accepted—because I wasn't Italian.

"Mama Mia," he would say. "What am I going to do with you?"

The second thing to overcome with The Butcher was that I was in Eglin for a white-collar crime. He said that guys like me were phonies because we had to rob people with a pen; we didn't have the courage to put a gun in their faces. He also said that my pen was more lethal than his gun, anyway. To hear The Butcher talk, vice could almost sound like virtue as long as it was done out in the open, above board—and you were Italian.

The Butcher became the object of daily prayer in our prison fellowship group. He had been in front of the parole board on several occasions, and each time they had said they weren't ready to review his case and asked him to come back in twenty-four months. In four or five months he was scheduled to see the board again.

All the time Joe was at Eglin he was a visible part of that compound. He had become a Christian at the Atlanta pen. He read the Word every morning. Any time you visited his cube the Bible was open to a new section. His ministry was to those younger men who felt too big for their own good. He was "Mr. Crime," and his words carried a lot of authority.

"Listen, Jesus was no punk," he would explain. "He could have copped out any time he wanted to, but he never did, and he never ratted out his friends. He was a stand-up guy."

It's amazing to realize how many different—yet effective—parts of the body Jesus has. Joe was and is to this day, I'm sure, a "stand-up guy" for the Lord he loves. Christ put an undeniable burden on my heart to write a letter on his behalf to the parole board. The hour before he was to meet them Joe prayed and then went back to his cube and fell asleep.

"What do I have to worry about?" he said. "Jesus is here with me, and I just show up to see what is going on." Incredibly, he was told that in four short months he would be free to go home.

I missed The Butcher after he left. Aside from the fellowship we shared, I wasn't able to get any good fruit!

Unquestionably, many inmates were initially drawn to our prayer fellowship group to see what Joe The Butcher was doing there. No one ever criticized him as he ordered other brothers to pray or as he launched into prayer himself, sounding somewhat like a motor boat pulling away from the dock.

We saw fascinating miracles. Orlando Cepeda, for example. I'll always remember his large, dark eyes and the pain they revealed. Others know Orlando as a star baseball player with the St. Louis Cardinals (where he was named Most Valuable Player in the National League one year) or with the Atlanta Braves or Boston Red Sox teams somewhat later. We prayed regularly for Orlando's family but especially for his mother, who took his incarceration very hard. Though Orlando expected to be released soon, his mother was falling deeper and deeper into depression. One week Orlando came into the prayer group, sat down, and wept like a baby. His mother's depression had worsened to the point that she could no longer care for herself. She was to be committed to a public mental institution in Puerto Rico—the next afternoon. We asked Orlando if we could lay hands on him and pray in proxy for his mother, and he agreed.

Five of us prayed, with all our hearts, for Orlando's mother to be healed instantly. When our prayer concluded, I suddenly acquired the worst headache of my life. My hands began to sweat. I figured that Satan must have gone to work, that a miracle was in process and he couldn't stand it. As I prayed aloud for Jesus to heal my hurting head, other brothers laid hands on me with prayer and bound Satan in the name of Jesus.

My head started to feel better, and I glanced at Orlando. He was still in tears. I had never been especially sensitive in discerning spirits, but I found myself walking over to him.

"Orlando, do you feel that your mother's problems have been caused by you? Do you feel guilty or unworthy?"

"Yes," he said through tears. "I know I have been a good son to her, but I can't help feeling personally responsible for what is happening." With that we prayed for Orlando again, asking Jesus to free him from the false spirits of guilt, condemnation, and unworthiness. Orlando was at last delivered from this torment. We could see the tranquility transform his face and relax his body. The Lord had sent the Comforter, who had taken control.

At our prayer group meeting the next day, Orlando could hardly wait to speak. "Last night my wife went to my mother's apartment to help her pack for the institution. She opened the door and found my mother as lucid as all of us in this room."

A murmur of "Praise the Lord" went around our circle. The Butcher's voice was no murmur; from him came a "Thank you, Jesus!" that rocked the room.

"I asked my wife when this happened," Orlando continued. "Figuring the time change between here and Puerto Rico, it had to be *the very time* we prayed for her."

Chuck,* another sweet-spirited fellow, came into our prayer group through "divine accident." Returning to my barracks one afternoon, I saw this nice-looking young man I recognized as new in the facility. He looked sad and completely alone. I introduced myself, and soon we were talking.

In the course of our talk, I shared with him about Jesus. And amazingly enough, by the end of our conversation, Chuck had invited Christ into his life.

Secretly, I was extremely proud of myself. After all, I had obeyed the call of God's Spirit and made myself available to Chuck. Not only that, but look how well I'd directed the conversation! I came to the conclusion that I had helped "close the deal" for the Lord.

Then Chuck burst my bubble. "I can't wait to phone my mother," he exclaimed. "My whole life will be different now. Mom's a Christian. She has prayed for my salvation every day for the past twenty years."

I felt very foolish. I had been ready to take credit for this conversion, having spent an hour of my time with Chuck.

He went on to say that his brother and sister-in-law had talked with him about faith in Christ numerous times since they had become Christians six years ago.

I left Chuck, returned to my cube, and opened the Bible. I read of Jesus riding into Jerusalem on a donkey. People lining the streets applauded and waved palm branches. I thought of my conversation with Chuck and smiled to myself. *Boy, that donkey probably thought the applause was for him!*

Life with the prayer group continued on a day-to-day, crisis-to-crisis basis. One of the brothers learned his wife had been raped by a motorcycle gang. Another man lost two children in an accident. Some men learned their wives were unfaithful; others found themselves faced with divorce proceedings.

Those troubles were real and affected us all. When the group got to a low ebb, however, you could count on The Butcher to stand up and tell the guys what babies they were. He knew how to snap people out of their pity parties:

"Youse guys wouldn't make it for a week in Atlanta. You have it so good here you can't imagine, and you walk around with your heads down. Fine examples you set for your families. They're the ones who have it rough. You know you're gonna be fed, have clean sheets on the bed. You don't have a problem in the world. Your wives probably don't have enough money to get along, have to work full time and take care of the kids. Then what happens? Mama Mia, you get on the phone sounding depressed and drive them crazy! What does The Butcher have to do, rap you on the side of the head?"

Our periods of learning were made up of tears, laughter, depression, joy, but through it all, growth. We always agreed, despite our differences, when it came to praying for a child. As a group, we adopted several children. Our hearts went out to one child in particular.

Can you imagine being in prison and learning that your three-year-old son was dying of cancer? That man felt so helpless and suffered such despair that, without the fellowship of Christ, there's no telling what he would have done.

Our prison fellowship prayer group contacted the warden and insisted that he call Washington to obtain furlough privileges for a father whose baby was given only three months to live. The prayers that went up for that family! The superintendent worked with the parole board in Washington to get that father an early release.

Our brother left us, but we continued to pray for God to heal that little boy. His dad was home for four months before Jesus took the child home. He wrote to describe the final weeks; the letter tore us apart.

Praying for that child for over a year unified the prayer group, and his death was devastating to us, especially those who were new in the Lord. We'd prayed for a miracle, however, and I had to believe that God heard and answered. Our brother had begun to reconstruct his life at home. And his last letter brought news that they were expecting a baby.

While I was at Eglin, Mother died.

Though her health had been failing for many years, it was hard to imagine that her life could stop. She had been a fighter, wrestling with life every day, from the time I'd known her. And life had been so difficult for Mother—from poor to rich to poor again and the losses of her friends, hopes, and dreams.

Her last will and testament stated that she was to be cremated, with her ashes spread over the ocean. She especially requested that there be no funeral service. This made sense; Mother had alienated most of the important people in her life. In spreading her ashes, she obviated having to be buried next to Dad—a man she never forgave. *Gritty to the end, weren't you, Mother?* I thought, marveling at the toughness of this tiny lady, who'd continually been my adversary—and my mother.

When I told my case manager about Mother's death and requested time to be with my family, he had to turn me down. "I spoke to the people in administration," he told me, "and they said, 'no funeral, no furlough.' "

"You mean that if Mother had decided to have a funeral I would have been allowed a five-day furlough, yet since she didn't, I don't get any leave at all?

"That's about it. Bureau of Prisons policy," he replied.

Mother willed her entire estate to Rosemary. Her legacy to me took the form of intangibles, some good and some bad. People say I inherited her sense of humor, for which I'm grateful. She was one of the funniest, most charming, and gracious hostesses I've known. When her mood was up, she was a joy. But when it was foul, well, she wasn't known as the "War Empress" for nothing. Another thing she had left me was the approach to life that helped me get into prison:

"Remember, Steve, a buck is your best friend." Mother and I had shared several negative qualities, including the ability to carry a grudge indefinitely.

In a few days we would celebrate Easter. Emotions ran in extremes in our prayer group. For some, the separation from family was nearly unbearable. For others, it was a high time; we looked forward to the sunrise service we had received permission to conduct. Chaplain Castillo would meet us on the sand behind the dorm buildings and lead us in a worship service as the sun rose.

I had decided not to mention anything to the group about Mother's passing or the institution's decision not to permit me to be with my family at this time. I was afraid it would only be opportunity for bitterness and anger, thus dampening the joy and holiness of Easter Sunday.

After that Sunday, though, Harvey told me over the phone that it was important for me to commit Mother's spirit to God in prayer. I didn't understand what that meant—I'm still not sure what it means—but I did as she suggested. In prayer, I committed Mother's spirit into God's keeping, expressing hope that she and Dad could have eternal life in heaven.

It is useless to theologize on this point. To my knowledge, neither of my parents ever came to a faith in Christ. But God granted me peace that day, and how God deals with the souls of other people isn't up to me. Once again, I was powerless and even more aware of how everything ultimately comes from the Lord's hand.

Dr. James Monroe, pastor of the First Baptist Church

of Fort Walton Beach, often visited our group. Dr. Monroe is a man who loves God, and he loved each of us; in fact, his church adopted us. Dr. Monroe arranged for baptismal candidates from the prison to receive a believer's baptism at his church. He held revival services in the prison for a week each year, showed us slides from his most recent trip to the Holy Land, and sent a stream of wonderful musicians and Bible teachers to encourage and train us as Christians.

In turn, Dr. Monroe often arranged to transport us to First Baptist, where our fellowship choir would sing and give testimonies. Then there would be a time of fellowship, homemade food cooked by the ladies of the church, and the warmth that comes from being received into the body of Christ and made welcome.

Like the other inmates, I received several unforgettable blessings from God during my prison term. But knowing and loving that godly servant heads the list.

Loving, serving, praying, forgiving, learning—what lessons our motley group of men was to experience together! Sometimes, even now, I think of those times, thank God once again, and pray for brothers incarcerated at Eglin whom I've never known.

There we all learned that the Lord's grace abounds, even in one of Satan's prime breeding grounds: America's prisons.

# Chapter 17

# CRISIS IN SPRINGFIELD

During the twenty-minute ride to the airport, my pain became unbearable. I asked for and received permission to lie down in the rear of the empty prison station wagon. An inmate driver and the prison doctor, beside him on the front seat, were taking me to a private airport.

"Doc," a physician's assistant was convinced that I had medical problems beyond his scope. Just what his scope was, none of us knew. The story had been circulated that he had once treated an inmate for jaundice for three months before noticing that the man was Chinese. He even had problems keeping potted plants alive in the infirmary. Actually, the doctor's poor attitude accomplished a great deal in terms of preventative medicine; five hundred inmates were scared to death of getting sick. But my X-rays had shown that the neck and arm pains I suffered were not merely subjective. I'd have to transfer to Springfield prison for treatment.

Since some airlines were striking, the prison had chartered a private plane to transport me. Had they not considered this trip an emergency, I'd have taken a series of prison planes and buses, shackled the entire way. I was grateful to miss that experience, as well as the series of jails in which I would have been held pending various connections.

When we landed, we discovered there was no guard waiting to escort me to the prison. Since the pilot needed to return to Florida without delay, I found myself in the strange position of bidding him farewell and phoning the prison for instructions.

"Steve who?" someone asked. "What are you talking about?" It seemed that a week earlier, Doc had requested that I be accepted for possible surgery; the request had been approved, but my arrival date had never been confirmed. I explained that the pilot had left me at the airport and jokingly mentioned that unless they picked me up I'd be willing to fly to Mexico for the winter since Eglin didn't expect me back for a while. My humor was appreciated, but they assured me a guard would be on the way.

The guard was the tight-lipped type. I attempted to ask a few questions. "Would you say I have anything to fear pertaining to my personal safety here?"

"Just keep your nose clean," he replied. "Everything will be okay." For some reason I didn't feel reassured.

Springfield prison appeared over the knoll of a nearby hill, and its very appearance confirmed every horrible thing I'd heard about the place the past few weeks. Towers that housed armed guards rose ominously to the forefront. The entire place was bordered by a high brick wall with double rows of barbed wire as added security.

First I was taken to the receiving room, where I was strip-searched, given new prison clothing, then pushed into a holding cell. There I waited while they readmitted an inmate who several weeks earlier had attempted to commit suicide by swallowing lye. They had taken him to a local hospital, and he was returning with tubes still protruding from his stomach.

From the opposite direction came a stretcher holding the body of an inmate who had recently expired. A blanket covered his face, and the guards ignored everything about the body except for papers that had to be filled out.

Next came a busload of shackled prisoners who arrived from other facilities. They were processed—searched, photographed—while I waited.

I asked the guard if he would hand me my Bible through the bars, but he refused, claiming that it hadn't been examined yet and told me I needed to be quiet and not hassle anyone.

Soon they assigned me to a building, floor, and hospital bed, and I was escorted to my new home. Portions of the prison housed up to three hundred occupants at any time—incorrigibles who came from prisons around the country. Many could not be handled by their guards, so they had been sent there to be segregated and medicated with Thorazine to calm them.

The rest of the population numbered about five hundred and were mostly transients. We came from other prisons and were there for medical or psychological problems (or both)—some real, some imagined. Certain inmates from Marion prison, for example, said they'd been there for ten years and wanted a change of scenery. Feigning back problems allowed them to leave long enough to catch at least a glimpse of some late-model cars and see how the world had changed.

That evening I phoned home after waiting in line for the single available pay phone for more than two hours to tell my concerned wife that everything looked fine and she was not to worry. I sounded more convinced of that than I actually felt.

Bizarre experiences and characters awaited me at this place. The second evening in my new home I walked in on a rape when I entered the showers; I exited quickly. I soon learned that no one got underneath his covers in bed without untucking both sides. That way you could escape an attack from either side without delay.

The fellow in the bed next to mine had pornographic tattoos all over his body, "Love" and "Hate" tattooed on the fingers of each hand, and a red and purple likeness of a devil that curled from the muscle on his left arm down to a point on the back of his hand. He wore mirrored sunglasses at all times.

"You a preacher?" he asked, taking note of my Bible. "No," I answered, launching him into a long, hostile monologue wherein this roommate proceeded to tell me about his plans to escape, catch his wife and her lover, tie them up, and douse them with gasoline. He described how he'd laugh as they burned to a crisp. A Bible placed in his room during a stay in solitary confinement had been his only diversion, and he had asked Christ into his life. After his release from solitary, he had committed his fifth murder; he now considered himself a Christian murderer.

Nobody was in a hurry here. It took me five days to see a doctor, and they took their time administering a series of tests. Eventually my treatment included traction for several days and instructions to return to Eglin, with directions not to lift anything heavier than twenty-five pounds. My weight was heading down to 148 pounds, significantly less than the 182 I'd carried on my six-foot-one frame when I first entered Eglin.

I heard that they had fresh eggs on the menu that first Sunday and made sure I found the mess hall. It took twenty minutes to reach the head of the line, and as I headed toward a table, a hand came from nowhere, took my plate off the tray, dumped its contents onto another plate, and then put my empty plate back on its tray. Startled, I looked up at the man who belonged to the hand. He must have been six feet five, with the arms of a sumo wrestler. I simply smiled and said that I hoped he would enjoy his eggs.

I looked around the mess hall as I ate my toast and drank the C-ration coffee. My eyes settled at last on a figure I can only describe as a walking nut factory—"the general."

He stood at attention, his eyes straight ahead, his tray held chest high. As the line moved ahead he took the smartest of military steps forward. At the steam line, he saluted the inmates behind the counter. All eyes in the place were riveted on him as he left the line and looked for a place to sit.

He crossed the huge room and marched directly to my table. He came to a halt, clicked his heels twice, and motioned with his head toward an empty chair opposite me. He didn't say a word.

"Sure, sit down. It's not taken," I said. He sat with his back erect and began to eat a "square meal." Any military school graduate can tell you about a square meal: bring food straight up from your plate to mouth height, then straight across to your mouth, and then reverse the process to return the fork to the plate. The face looks forward with eyes straight ahead, never looking to the left or right.

All this the general did but with one interesting variation; he didn't use any eating utensils. Egg yolk dripped between his fingers, and he seemed oblivious to all that surrounded him. "Excuse me," I said, departing in haste. Apparently he didn't hear me.

The next time I went to the mess hall, the general showed up again. I watched him salute the people along the wall. As he marched through the line, something told me he'd present himself at my table. Sure enough, he zigzagged his way past hundreds of others, crossed the room, and searched out the far corner where I sat. Again, the head motion toward the empty seat, the repeated heel clicking. I nodded okay, and he sat down.

This time the "square meal" business involved spaghetti and meat sauce—with his fingers, of course, putting yesterday's egg exhibition to shame. Soon meat sauce covered his face, hands, shirt, and half the table. His head wasn't in much better shape as he'd run his fingers through his hair in an attempt to keep it out of his face.

I decided I wouldn't leave this time. Nothing, including the general's insanity, would prevent me from eating my Italian cuisine. No doubt the general couldn't understand a word I'd say but it gave me courage to speak. "General, someday I'd like to invite you to my mother-in-law's house for dinner. I know Marjory would love to meet you. I'll tell her about you, but I know she won't believe me."

The general paid no attention whatever. "You know, general," I continued, "I'm a Christian. And the Lord says in his Word that if we do a good turn for the least of his people, we have done it for him. It seems that you almost qualify as one of his 'least.' I know God loves you and I do too, but you're a disaster around spaghetti!" I bade the general good-bye and left the table, but he didn't seem to notice.

The same thing happened the next day, though I'd changed locations. "General," I said, "we really have to stop meeting this way. I think my wife is on to us." There was no response from his side of the table, but it didn't matter. I was playing the scene for my own entertainment. When I excused myself from the table I received a sloppy salute from a hand garnished with meat sauce and Thousand Island dressing. The thought crossed my mind that it looked as though the inmates had taken over the asylum.

I returned to my section, lay on the bed, and began reading my Bible. This brought some comments, as usual: "How come you're a Christian, yet you're in here with the rest of us?" I was getting used to that question.

Several yards away, some inmates stood around the bed of a garrulous old-timer who loved to spin a yarn. Usually I paid no attention to their conversation, but today I heard my name. My ears perked up. Most of what they were saying about me was not complimentary. Some of them agreed that jailhouse religion indicated weakness in a man. After all, I had gotten myself into trouble. Why wasn't I man enough to get myself out of trouble without asking God to do it for me? Obviously, my continual Bible reading bugged them.

The old-timer took a different attitude, though. He believed religion was okay and that if a person wanted it and it helped him "do time" easier, then that was all right. Then he said the saddest thing I'd ever heard:

"You know, I'm sixty-three years old and don't think I ever had someone pray for me."

Without thinking, I got out of bed and walked toward the semi-hostile gathering. I passed the others and stood directly in front of the old-timer. "I heard what you just said and want you to know I'll pray for you right now," I offered.

He began to cry. The crowd instantly dispersed, leaving us alone. I asked the old inmate to name his needs and requests, and after that brief checklist we began to pray. Our prayer was intense, earnest, and unrestrained. The Holy Spirit seemed to permeate the whole room. The man was eager to ask Jesus into his life.

Later that evening, another fellow came by. He must have been six feet five, and I recognized the arms of the man who'd taken the eggs off my plate that first day in the mess hall. He had moved into our section several days earlier, and he didn't appear to be Jesus's biggest fan, judging from his vocabulary.

This mountain of a fellow acted nervous. He shifted his weight from one foot to the other. "Uh, Preacher, will you, uh—I mean—will you pray for me?"

"Of course I will." I asked him his name.

"It's Charles.*" As we held hands and prayed, tears streamed down his face.

"Do you know who Jesus is, Charles?"

"Yes, he's God's Son."

"Is there any reason you shouldn't ask him into your life right now?"

"I dunno."

"Let's pray again, but this time after I get through saying a prayer, I want you to repeat some words after I say them. Okay?"

"Okay, Preacher."

A few minutes later Charles had become my brother in Christ. We found a *Good News for Modern Man* Bible in a magazine rack, and Charles read it faithfully. He had a true hunger for spiritual food. I prayed for Charles for some time.

When my myelogram tests showed that I didn't need surgery, I was assigned to another wing. The guys gave me a brief wave and a "Good-bye, Preacher." I never saw any of them again.

That evening I walked to the mess hall from a different direction than usual and at a later time. Upon entering the line, I saw the general already seated. *It's one thing for him to pick me out,* I thought. *No one can blame me for that. But if I pick him out to sit with, everyone will believe I'm as crazy as he is!* I sat by myself some twenty tables away.

Suddenly the general rose to his feet, picked up his tray, and with great military bearing, came to my table. Our meal went quietly, but he spread dinner all over the place. I couldn't tell if he had an itch or was trying to stuff tuna casserole up his nose.

I returned to my new quarters glad I could get out of this crazy house, no matter what sort of transportation the Bureau of Prisons provided. That evening, however, I discovered that my urine was red as wine. It was similar to times before when I had passed kidney stones. But I'd never had this much bleeding.

What if jouncing about on the prison bus caused the stone to start moving? I could imagine being in incredible pain with no access to medical attention and in the company of disinterested and unsympathetic guards. That evening I placed an emergency request to see the doctor.

The next day, X-rays showed nothing. The day after that, the doctor scheduled another test. I was told that since I was over forty years old and nothing had shown up on the X-rays, there was a 40 percent certainty that I'd developed bladder cancer.

That night at dinner I hardly ate at all. The general sat there, eating with that distinctive two-fisted style of his, and I related my despair about the possibility of discovering bladder cancer in a place like this prison. I expected no loving bedside manner here, of course. The general apparently heard none of my remarks, though he saluted me occasionally.

In bed that evening, the tears flowed. A yard light sent a beam through the barred window and illuminated my pictures of Blake and Harvey. I prayed like I never had before. I did not want to die.

First, I begged God to spare my life. My prayers did not result in peace, however. Next, I tried to arouse God's sympathies. "Lord, I want Harvey to have the sort of life she deserves. We're a Christian family now, so please add years to my life as you did with Hezekiah, so Harvey and I might grow old together." I mentioned my little boy and how I wanted to do the things with him my father had never taken the time to do with me.

But the torment continued with no peace in sight. At three in the morning my pillow was drenched with tears. I had been at it since ten in the evening. Finally, out of sheer exhaustion, I gave up. "Lord, I hoped you wanted me to live a long life. If so, I'm yours and I'll witness to your glory until the day you take me home. But if you want me here for just a short lifetime, I'm still yours. With your help I'll witness despite illness or pain."

With that, peace came, and I fell asleep immediately.

The next morning when I awoke I was convinced that everything was fine. I felt so refreshed and joyous that I asked God to confirm these feelings if they truly were from him. An inmate wearing surgical greens and a mask came for me with a gurney. He was calling in a Cuban accent: "Praise de Lord! Praise de Lord, where is Brother Lawson?"

"Over here!" I half shouted.

"Praise de Lord! He is so faithful!" he chirped. "Don't worry, Brother Lawson. The Lord has a lot of plans for you."

We prayed there in the hall. I knew that God had sent this angel to minister especially to me.

In surgery, the problem turned out to be a kidney stone, after all; it was retrieved with little difficulty. The stone simply hadn't shown up in the X-ray.

That afternoon I explained to the warden that slow prison transportation might cause me to miss my parole board meeting that was coming up at Eglin. Within hours, what I consider another miracle occurred: I was given permission to travel from Springfield the next afternoon via commercial bus to Eglin.

Dinner that evening was considerably better than the night before. I was bursting with the good occurrences of the last twenty-four hours, but I had learned that it's wise not to share such things in prison. Others either aren't interested or could be envious of your good fortune. However, I had the perfect dinner companion, one with whom I could share my good news. The general, as usual, didn't get envious or make any comments. I could tell him anything I liked. When he crossed the room to sit with me, I smiled.

"By all means, general," I encouraged. Soon our usual one-way conversation had begun. "Well, general, this is our last dinner. Tomorrow I leave this zoo and return to Eglin."

At that, the general looked directly at me and said, "I'm sorry to hear that. You've been a wonderful sport to put up with all my crap, and I apologize if I've turned your stomach."

I was in shock. The general continued to eat his square meal for the benefit of others sitting around us.

"Do you mean to tell me you're not crazy?" I asked.

"Of course not. Actually, you're more nuts than I am. Why would you sit with someone like me and continually converse with someone who'd never answer you?"

"General, you have a point there, although it's a little late to bring any sort of logic to our relationship. Tell me, though, why do you do all this, anyway?"

He told me he'd graduated from a well-known school of finance and then enlisted in the Marines. "The government wants me on about 105 counts," he said, "and I'm trying to convince everyone I'm spaced out due to battle fatigue."

"Hey, that's your business," I told him. "I wish you all the luck in the world. But you must be stone crazy to have pulled this over on me night after night."

"I'll miss you," he answered. With that he saluted me, scooped up his mashed potatoes, combed them through his hair, and gave me another three rapid salutes.

When I returned to my section I received the message to report to the clothing room immediately. It was time to be outfitted for my civilian return to Eglin. I was given black socks and shoes, undershorts, and a T-shirt. Then, in a flash of warped humor, the guard reached for a lime green polyester leisure suit with a royal blue shirt featuring a print of lime green palm trees. He handed it to me straight-faced. *Maybe he didn't have a sense of humor, after all.* No, I could not make another selection. I was in prison, he informed me. And if I didn't like the way things were done, I should have thought of that before I committed my crime.

The next day I was given a ride to the bus depot. Although I looked disreputable, I was a "free" man for the duration of this trip. No guards or shackles. Just another traveler—with very bad taste in clothing.

Springfield had been quite an excursion. I had spent a lot of time reading the Bible—up to ten hours some days. I had encountered some strange people and seen God's grace touch a couple of lives.

But most importantly, I had entered yet another dimension in Christ. I had faced the possibility of cancer and death and learned to yield even that to God's hands. I would never forget that all-night vigil of prayer and struggle. God had managed to bring me new growth there in the maximum security prison of Springfield.

# Chapter 18

# MAN'S LAW, GOD'S GRACE

I had ignored the parole board for quite some time because I had received a "regular" adult sentence known as an "A" sentence, which dictated that I'd stay under the judge's authority and serve at least one-third of my prison term before parole consideration. This meant that I had to serve at least thirty-two months before becoming eligible for parole board consideration or even to be eligible for a furlough.

Soon after I reported to Eglin, my attorneys, who believed my sentence excessive for a white-collar, nonviolent crime, submitted a Rule 35 to Judge Warner. This rule allows a judge to reconsider a sentence upon receipt of new information. It seemed to me that most inmates applied for a Rule 35, as most believed they'd been unfairly sentenced and sought reduced sentences. I believed that a judge knew the facts before he passed a sentence and was therefore unlikely to change his mind.

Despite my intellectual reasoning, I had high hopes. I had read newspaper accounts of seven-year and eight-year sentences being handed down for such heinous crimes as rape and murder. Harvey had asked our friends in the Christian community to write to the judge on my behalf.

There was no new information in my case for the judge to consider. Nevertheless, we submitted the Rule 35 with the hope—certainly not the expectation—that he might change the sentence.

Miraculously, he did just that. Judge Warner did not change the eight-year factor, but he did designate my sentence as B-2, instead of regular adult, which meant that I could see the parole board at any time and should they see fit, serve less than the mandatory sentence less time off for good behavior. Harvey and I rejoiced at this. The judge's action implied that he might have leveled too harsh a sentence after all. Surely the parole board would notice that.

I informed my case worker that I'd like to see the parole board on their next visit. It appeared to be impossible since they already had a full schedule. I would have to wait for their next visit in another two months. Meanwhile, I could visit the law library and learn how I could best represent myself. Though my attorney had offered to represent me at that hearing, I wanted to speak to the board myself.

In the course of my research, I discovered a number of factors in my favor:

1. I had made restitution to many of my former clients. I had paid them back as well as given them a 40 percent profit.
2. I voluntarily separated myself from the crime by calling it to the government's attention.

3. I saved the government considerable expense by pleading guilty rather than prolonging the trial procedure.

4. There were special considerations too. Blake was feeling the effects of my absence, and we would submit a psychologist's report to that effect. Harvey was encountering financial hardships. Also, I had documented proof that my back condition required a physician's care.

5. I was not the same man who committed the crimes. I was truly repentant for my past.

6. The institutional-adjustment report from my case worker was favorable, recommending that I be granted positive parole consideration.

I readied myself in every way possible for meeting the parole board. Our prayer group prayed for me daily. I continued reading the Bible and praying.

I entered the hearing room that day feeling thankful already. This time I would argue my case myself rather than have lawyers represent me. My version had never been given clearly in court since I had pleaded guilty.

Two parole board members sat behind a long table, with my case worker positioned to the side. They clicked a tape recorder on and then read a litany of the original proceedings. At last they began questioning me directly, and from the tone of their queries, I could tell they were uninformed about my case. My heart began to sink as I tried to clarify certain aspects of their questions. After a while I was given the opportunity to speak freely with uninterrupted time. I reviewed all the points I'd listed before, all that seemed favorable to my case. I ended by stating that I was a new person in Jesus Christ, truly repentant, and that the past eight months of incarceration had been used profitably in growing in my Christian faith through reading the Word of God. By the end of my discourse I had begun to weep.

Without changing expression, the board asked me to wait in the hall while they deliberated. I was nervous but prayerfully confident; I felt sure that the Holy Spirit had given me the right words to say.

Back inside, I was told: "Mr. Lawson, we reviewed the circumstances of your crimes and balanced them against the things you said today. We reviewed your institutional report, which is quite good. The aggravating aspect of your crimes, however, is that you signed a consent decree in 1974 and violated that court order by breaking the security laws again. Therefore, we recommend that you serve sixty-four months."

It took me only a moment to compute this. "That's my eight-year sentence less time off for good behavior, isn't it?"

"Yes, it is. Do you have any other questions, Mr. Lawson?"

"No, I don't. I guess I'll just have to depend on the Lord to somehow make each of those months a blessing."

"Well, good luck to you. That will be all."

I left the building nauseated and in a state of shock. How could I phone Harvey and tell her I'd remain in prison for more than five years? How do I tell my precious son that I'll be coming home—when he's eleven?

In the chapel, I shared this news with Bill Bevers,* the chaplain's clerk. Bill loved God's Word and could recall it when a person needed it most. And he ministered to me with gentle, caring words and comforting Scriptures that restored my battered spirit.

Scriptures like Ephesians 6:12: "For our struggle is not against flesh and blood, but against the rulers, against the authorities, against the powers of this dark world and against the spiritual forces of evil in the heavenly realms." If so, then what had happened? We knew it wasn't the Lord's will for me to remain in prison sixty-four months.

You may be thinking, *Why not?* Simply, I *knew* that God did not want me there. There was a quiet confidence of that deep in my spirit.

Other Scriptures came to mind then: "And we know that in all things God works for the good of those who love him, who have been called according to his purpose" (Romans 8:28). And "Never will I leave you; never will I forsake you" (Hebrews 13:5).

Bill helped me to pray for God's peace, for the assurance that God was still in control of my life, and for blessings on Harvey and Blake—and preparation for Harvey to receive this news.

Harvey's reaction was evidence of God's intervention. "Praise the Lord," she said quietly after one long breath. My wife then proceeded to offer me comfort, even when she had just received a sentence far rougher than my own. She assured me of her love for God, of her and Blake's love for me, and that they would be there, waiting, no matter how long I was in prison. And she reminded me that the troubles of the present were nothing to compare to the happy times we'd have later.

There were two other sets of reactions, however, to the parole board's decision. Within the prison, there was, frankly, a glorification of my craftiness and wrongdoing. I'd become a sort of hero. Because of the new sentencing regulations enacted before my confinement, I had one of the longer sentences at Eglin. The parole board had just clobbered me, meaning to those on the inside that I was a legitimate and stand-up guy. I surely hadn't turned over evidence on another to lessen my sentence. Also, if the board had me "maxing out" for a white-collar crime on an already stiff sentence, I must have been one smart cookie on the outside. My crime must have been big. Inside Eglin, I'd become officially "okay." Even The Butcher looked at me with new respect.

Outside, however, the mood was different. "What had happened?" they asked on the phone and by letter. Was there something I hadn't told my brothers in Christ? Had I really come to grips with my guilt and the nature of my crimes? Also, some suggested, since the Lord hadn't answered our prayers, obviously I must be doing something wrong. For some reason perhaps I wasn't meeting the conditions needed to receive a blessing. Letters offered Scriptures and lovingly suggested that I reassess my relationship with God.

The doubts of these fellow believers hurt, of course, but I could understand their viewpoint. I wished I were innocent of the crimes I'd committed. That would establish a wonderful rallying point for my prayer partners since it would be easy to pray that justice be done. It's much harder to admit that justice *was* done and that I was praying instead for mercy.

Eventually, my Christian brothers and sisters were solidly behind me again. And although we didn't see it coming, the Lord was about to use them in ways none of us had visualized. Carbon copies of letters began to arrive—letters that had been sent to the parole board in support of my regional appeal. They were requesting en masse that my sentence be cut. Soon I'd lost count of the number. After several months of this, the voice of my case worker came over the loudspeaker, summoning me to his office.

He had received an order from the regional parole board offices in Atlanta stating that they fully agreed with the aggravating aspect of my crime but nevertheless saw no reason to go outside the sentencing guidelines formulated by the federal government. These guidelines are based on the dollar amount of the crime along with many other factors. According to this formula, my incarceration should have been anywhere between twenty-four and thirty-six months. Consequently, the regional parole board had reduced my sentence from sixty-four months to thirty-six!

It was a great moment that afternoon when I shared my good news with our prayer group and felt their joy in how God had come to my help. Each of these men had encouraged me and prayed for me. Now, we kneeled all together and asked God's blessings on those men and women on the outside who had given their love so generously on my behalf.

*Chapter 19*

# PRISON FELLOWSHIP

John Wilkin and I sat amidst our prayer group. Every man there could have been envious, yet they rejoiced for us. After all, we were the two guys of twelve who were picked out of an entire federal prison system that contains three hundred thousand to attend a two-week paid seminar conducted by Prison Fellowship. We would be free men for the entire time, operating within an honor system. There'd be no guards, no bedside checks or counts.

From Eglin, John and I flew into Pittsburgh with a two-hour layover in Atlanta. Harvey and Blake were there for a visit that was amazingly natural. It became obvious, as Blake and I played, that the miles and our separation hadn't diminished our love and affection.

It was the same with Harvey and me. I was so proud of her. She handled her challenges with a magnificent attitude. Indeed, many have said Harvey's daily walk was an example to them; they claimed that they never saw her with bowed head or unsmiling face. She praised God for her blessings, showed a forgiving spirit, and rejoiced rather than complained. She was serving as both mother and father to a lively youngster who needed quality time, and I knew that Blake's great attitude toward me stemmed from the fact that his mother never displayed anything less.

As she remembers, "I watched Blake and Stephen play and enjoy each other. It was a wonderful tonic for me every bit as much as it was for Blake. Stephen was the same person I had always known and admired, yet he was different. He was stronger and had more leadership qualities than I had ever seen in him before. His faith was strong; he buoyed me when he called or wrote. I felt his strength much more now than I had in the old days when the world said we had everything.

"Many friendships from that affluent past had vanished. However, some of our old friends did care enough to call— at least the men did. Three married men who had known Stephen and me for years offered to help me through the lonely times I was obviously experiencing by suggesting we meet for dinner or that I travel with them while they were out of town on business. I didn't mention any of this to Stephen; it would only have increased his torment. For the time being I would keep it to myself. I wasn't bitter, just disappointed. I could see how much these men needed a living God in their lives too, just as Stephen and I had. But I didn't feel that taking them on as ministry projects was part of God's plan for my life.

"Stephen had to live one day at a time, and so would I. We had discussed the dynamics of prison life—aspects that were his and his alone to handle. And without him at home, I was in a prison too. There were some things that were only mine to handle."

At the Pittsburgh airport, John and I joined seven other inmates from elsewhere around the country. We piled into a Prison Fellowship van and began the two hours-long drive to the Ligonier Valley Study Center in Stahlstown, Pennsylvania. There we were housed two to a room in a beautiful chalet with suites opening into a great room with a huge fireplace and roaring fire.

This is where we had our classes and enjoyed fellowship while relishing our freedom.

We were as fascinated with the staff as they were with us. This was their first experience with inmates, and they were genuinely excited to have us as guests for the week. Sometimes we ate in the dining hall, but often we were invited into the teachers' homes, where we enjoyed delicious meals amid warm family surroundings.

It wasn't all study. There was a ski trip at a nearby lodge—a hilarious excursion—the highlight being my rather spectacular crash into a tool shed. The laughter and kidding I took that day were unmerciful!

Another evening we visited a Pizza Hut—an unimaginable treat for guys who'd eaten prison food as long as we had. We ordered the works, ate like condemned men, and luxuriated in simply sitting at a table and enjoying table service.

"I hope everything was okay," our waitress commented as she presented our checks.

"Great!" answered one of the guys.

"Are you men from around these parts?"

"No, we're in town one week and staying at the Ligonier Valley Study Center."

"That's nice. Is it a convention? What business are you in?"

"You might say we work for the government," said Al,* who was doing time for second-degree murder.

"Well, enjoy your stay. I hope the service was okay."

"Ma'am, I want you to know something very honestly," Al continued. "This is the best service I've had in the past ten years!"

As our waitress floated away, thrilled over the compliment, we couldn't begin to stifle our laughter.

Our week at Ligonier passed all too quickly. We'd become a close-knit group by now, bound together by good teaching, Bible study, prayer, and fellowship. It was hard to say good-bye. We chipped in and bought red roses for the ladies on staff; they were tearfully given and tearfully received.

The second week was spent in Washington, DC, where we were housed at the Holy Name Monastery. We had private rooms and use of the upstairs kitchen. How wonderful to have snack privileges! In the daytime we studied. Each evening, however, we visited various area churches, where we gave personal testimonies and fellowshipped with local congregations. I was treated to so many poultry dinners that even today I have a hard time passing a Kentucky Fried Chicken without having an overwhelming desire to witness.

That Sunday I gave my testimony at the Fourth Presbyterian Church in Bethesda, Maryland. Two thousand people attended each service, and a short part of my testimony was used on a local radio program. Days later, at our graduation ceremony, a man sought me out, threw his arms around me, and began to cry. He told me he had asked Jesus into his life many years earlier but for the past fifteen years had backslid and hardly ever visited church. My short testimony on the radio had brought him to his knees, and he had rededicated his life to God.

This story dumbfounded me. Upon my return to Eglin, however, I received many letters with similar reports. It made me realize how hungry people are to hear the good news, and it reminded me of two truths from Scripture: "Blessed is he who comes in the name of the LORD" (Psalm 118:26) and "The harvest is plentiful but the workers are few" (Matthew 9:37).

Harvey was able to join me for our final two days of the seminar. The Pattersons surprised us by giving Harvey a plane ticket to Washington, and our sweet friend Grace Kinser provided funds for our hotel room and miscellaneous expenses. Prison Fellowship had received permission from the Bureau of Prisons for husbands and wives to stay in a downtown Washington motel the last two days and provided free time within our schedules. Harvey and I took lovely walks in the snow and long lunches, where we could talk and catch up. We were amazed how, after thirteen years of marriage and the events of recent years, we still enjoyed one another so much.

It was hard to imagine, as we sat and talked, that I was a federal prisoner. Nothing seemed any different, yet in two days, we'd both return to our confinements.

Commencement exercises were emotional and unforgettable. I'd been chosen to give a three-minute overview of our two weeks in Washington and Ligonier but had not prepared any notes. Anyway, the snow was coming down hard; *attendance probably would be light.*

We walked into the church and found it jammed. People were seated in the aisles and in the choir loft, behind the pulpit. When the program began and I was introduced, I started my talk by saying that Chuck Colson had asked me to limit my remarks to three minutes.

"Well, I have no intention of doing that," I told them. "I'll speak as long as I'd like. After all, what can he do to me? Throw me in prison?"

Laughter and applause broke out everywhere. After a few moments of serious comments, I prepared to conclude my talk. At that moment, I noticed the look on Harvey's face. She was proud of me, a convict. Lord knows, I couldn't take my eyes off her.

"Honey, I love you so much," I said out loud. "There isn't a day that goes by that I don't thank God for you. I praise God that you have forgiven me, just as Jesus has done. I'm very blessed." Then, to the crowd, I continued, "I hope the Lord blesses each of you and the families you represent, richly and without limit—as he has mine."

That moment remains one of the highest in my life— when I was able to tell my wife publicly how much I loved and appreciated her.

The final ceremonies left us all at a high emotional level. We had been the center of attention and the object of many, many prayers. It would be hard to return to prison, where the distaste of the guards was so automatic.

Harvey and I departed for Atlanta the following morning. I wasn't due back at Eglin until evening, so we had a precious opportunity to attend church and worship together as a family. Following services, there were countless hellos, kisses, and handshakes during the fellowship period. The day passed joyously but all too quickly. At the airport later, I kissed Harvey and Blake good-bye and then boarded the plane to return to prison.

The flight to Eglin was quick, and soon one of the guards greeted me, asked how I'd enjoyed my two weeks, walked me to the back room, and began the customary strip search.

I was home.

*Chapter 20*

# FROM FAMILY TO FAMILY

n Washington I had met Norman Carlson, director of
the Bureau of Prisons, and Ben Malcolm, the National
Parole Board director. These men, impressed with Prison
Fellowship's accomplishments, always invited seminar
members to their offices for fellowship and questions. Ben
Malcolm particularly impressed me. When some of us
asked questions that permitted him to share his faith, he
seized the opportunity. His testimony was modestly told,
touching, and very believable.

We had also enjoyed getting to know Chuck Colson
and his wife, Patty. Chuck had offered his help in any way
possible during my appeal process. He could hardly have
known how timely his invitation was. One of the first things
I had to accomplish upon returning to Eglin was writing
my Washington appeal.

The day I sat down at the typewriter I ended up writing
pages of what I can only call my testimony. How else could
I explain to these people the change that had come to my
life? As a pauper in prison, I now had the peace and joy

that I never had as a "successful" man on the outside. I had failed miserably at success but had succeeded during failure because of Jesus's love for me. Why else would I be fit to be a free citizen, if Jesus Christ hadn't transformed me from the inside? When the project was finished, I decided that either the parole board would consider me crazy or the Holy Spirit would leap off the page and seize each of their hearts.

Next, I wrote a letter to all the people who had supported me for so long back home and to those new friends I'd met on my recent trip and requested assistance via their recommendations to the authorities.

Response to this letter was overwhelming. Letters written on my behalf poured into the various offices I'd named. Exactly ninety-four days from the time I posted my appeal, I was summoned to my case manager's office.

I looked at the form in his hand; I had received a twelve-month cut. Better than that, I had been recommended for a halfway house. A halfway house is a place in a person's hometown (in my case, an old Salvation Army boarding facility) where the prisoner stays for a set period of time. He is still a federal prisoner. He checks in at night but can hold a day job and gets weekends free. Thus, it is a halfway point between the person and real freedom, helping him to adjust to normal responsibilities and the outside world. I applied for a six-month halfway house, which is unusual— the customary time is a few weeks. But the six-month stay was approved. I would be able to spend Christmas with my family. In all, I would only be at Eglin for eighteen months.

Chaplain Castillo invited me to preach on my final Sunday, and I accepted with great pleasure. Harvey and Blake came down for the service and to say good-bye to friends we'd grown to love and respect. Carol,* a friend to all in the prison fellowship, from First Baptist, came to sing. Our choir also sang a few hymns, and Chaplain Castillo gave me an especially generous introduction. Following my sermon, several answered the invitation to ask Jesus to come into their lives. The service concluded with our Chapel Choir singing a personal favorite of mine: "Because He Lives, I Can Face Tomorrow." It was hard to say good-bye to the chaplain; we had logged a lot of prayer hours together.

Four days later came my last prayer group meeting. It was somewhat like a time of eulogy, with my brothers in Christ saying many touching things to me. It's amazing how, in such a harsh place as prison, the hearts of men can become tender and vulnerable. And I know it happens only by the grace of God.

Bill Beavers' sentence had been reduced to forty months, so I would soon see him on the outside too. The following morning I left on a commercial bus destined to arrive in Atlanta late that afternoon. I'd been given a bus ticket and thirty dollars in cash, compliments of my favorite Bureau of Prisons. But I passed on the green leisure suit; Harvey had provided clothes for this day: September 5, 1980.

As the bus droned out the miles toward Atlanta, I wondered what the future would bring. *Would I ever again be successful in business? Would people come to trust me? Would my life again be normal?* Time would tell. I knew that the

Lord's main concern was the condition of my heart. And my heart held the knowledge that I had been cleansed and forgiven.

The bus pulled into Atlanta on schedule, and soon I spotted Harvey and Blake at the top of the escalator. In moments I had reached them. The three of us crowded close for a corporate hug. After a long embrace with Harvey, I picked up my almost seven-year-old son, who was much taller and heavier than when I left.

Before anything else, I had to report to my halfway house. I was still a federal prisoner and would be for six more months. Processing went quickly at the halfway facility. They allowed me to check out for the weekend until eleven o'clock Sunday evening, which is the normal policy. I was free to go home!

Harvey drove, and Blake sat on my lap. "Stephen, it's over. It's really over, isn't it?" Harvey and I were both amazed that suddenly our lives seemed ordinary again.

"Yes, honey, it is."

"Daddy, I have a soccer game Saturday. It's the first game of the season. Will you come?"

"Are you kidding? I wouldn't miss it for anything!"

"When we get home will you play ball with me in the yard?" Blake was full of words now, news and questions he had stored up since I had left. Uncle Tim had gone with him for Father and Son Day at school the year before, but would I be there next time? Did I know he could catch a football now? He played soccer last year but didn't score any goals. Well, he did score, but it was the wrong goal. Could I coach him some?

I was conscious of every moment: Blake sitting on my lap, his little body next to mine; holding his hand while my other arm hugged his waist; feeling Harvey's hand resting on my left leg; sneaking little kisses on Blake's neck and cheek. God was already in the process of restoring those years the locusts had eaten away. Joel 2:25 says it clearly.

Traffic was heavy, but finally we exited the expressway. Out of words at last (and shushed somewhat by Harvey), Blake relaxed and became a third party to the conversation Harvey and I had begun. "How do you feel, Stephen? Is it strange?"

"Strangely enough, no. It's hard to believe that I'm just a few hours away from prison. I guess you and Blake are easy to come home to." I laughed, squeezing her hand.

My mind was operating on several levels at once. Outside, the old familiar streets slid by, looking just the same, yet different. My son, in my arms, was warm and solid yet older, heavier, his legs suddenly longer.

Harvey, though. Ah, she'd stayed the same. When I looked at her, I still saw the beautiful actress and dancer I met in New York City all those years ago.

"My background involved working as a ballet dancer, actress, model, and spokesperson," she once wrote. "I received praise for my performances and how I looked. I was always working towards the next big job around the corner. I was highly motivated to achieve, to be successful, and to be a winner in other people's eyes. My worth was based on my accomplishments. *No longer,* I thought."

"You look different," she said to me.

"What do you mean?"

"You have intensity in your face I never saw in the past. You have a furrow in your brow between your eyes too. And there's something different from the old Steve Lawson. I don't see the same bravado and self-confidence. But still, in another way, you're stronger than ever."

I listened, nodding in agreement, watching all that was happening on famous old Peachtree Road. Just two or three miles south of us, yet in another way so far behind us, was that funny high rise apartment where we'd begun our life together. We'd come a long way since the day we stood at the window, catching the end of the rainbow in the palms of our outstretched hands.

"Do you remember—" I started to ask, but then Harvey approached Vermont Road and began that final left turn as I caught my breath. We were moving into our driveway, and my eyes drank in every detail.

I saw the trees, the bushes, and every twig in our yard through rainbows created by my tears. Yellow ribbons were tied everywhere. They were just yellow ribbons, scraps of yellow to someone else, perhaps. But to my dazzled eyes that moment, they were a vision, even a revelation.

We were home. We were together. Suddenly I'd found something I never believed in before or thought was possible to see. I had found the pot of gold at the end of the rainbow.

# PART 2
# THE REST OF
# THE STORY

# Chapter 21

# MAKING SENSE OF LIFE AFTER PRISON

T he book of John assures us that all the books in the world
could not contain the acts of Jesus that fully show his mercy,
faithfulness, and love. I consider this book in your hands a
contract between God, Harvey, and me to be a book like that.
And I trust it will express how the gospel might be relived in
modern-day lives. In no way do we suggest that our lives are
more special than others. The only difference between your
story and ours is that you haven't written yours yet.

I returned home from prison in 1980. The book wasn't
published until 1992. *Daddy* had been well received, no
doubt due to Chuck Colson's foreword, which gave the
book instant recognition and validation. I was forty-three
when released from prison. Now I am seventy-six. Harvey
was thirty-seven then, now seventy-one. Blake was six,
now forty!

Attending a wedding reception at the Driving Club, my wife and I drifted toward the buffet table laden with shrimp, vegetables, roast beef, baked scallops, and shredded barbecue pork. After filling our plates, we looked for where we might sit at one of the round tables of ten surrounding the dance floor. We headed toward two open seats at a table that had just finished saying grace and asked if we might join them.

After introductions around the table, a man named Jim continued his prior discussion. "So when Chuck Colson said he was a born again Christian, I thought it was the most insane thing I'd ever heard. I never did like the guy, and his becoming a Christian was a leap of faith for *me* that I wasn't prepared to take because I could *not* give him the benefit of a doubt. Then he gets out of prison and starts Prison Fellowship. It didn't impress me one bit because I was convinced he wouldn't remain a Christian for the long term—certainly no longer than being a Christian seemed useful to him. But he stayed the course for over thirty-five years, and he won me over because after a time the only reasonable explanation of his changed life had to be Jesus Christ."

The others at the table nodded in agreement. The wife of another added, "Well, I read his book *Born Again* and thought the story was compelling, but I had the same reservations Jim did. At one time Colson was as far from being a Christian as anyone I could imagine. I can't tell you how many of those conversion stories I've read over the years. I think they're uplifting and totally believable. But I agree with Jim. I've often wondered how long these miraculous conversions last. Don't you agree," now looking at me, "that the credibility factor on these lives is something that's earned over a number of years?"

I hadn't met these people before, and they knew nothing of my background or book with a foreword by the very same Chuck Colson. "Yes," I said. "Come to think of it, I love the story of Zacchaeus's meeting Jesus and instantly repenting for the life he was leading. He promised to repay all those he had wronged, but we never hear about him again. I wonder how he lived the rest of his life after that treetop experience."

"Excellent point," Jim said. "Now take Lazarus. Jesus raised him from the dead. I wonder how the rest of his life demonstrated appreciation for what the Lord had done. How about Bartimaeus who received his sight? That was a nice enough miracle. What ever happened to that guy? After the miracle, we never run in to him again."

Then in short order the conversation turned back to the usual banter of such gatherings.

Jim's perspective sparked a deep curiosity with us. Had no other authors ever provided an update to a book they had written many years prior, sharing the miracle of their conversion with a matured, generational perspective? Where were they now in the faith? Our search didn't uncover anyone.

In reading *Daddy* again, Harvey grew excited over what she was sure the Holy Spirit was telling her. "Stephen, we need to update this book and share what the last thirty-four years after prison have been like. We need to share how the experience affected us spiritually, emotionally, and socially. There is a lot to tell that could help others who have experienced trauma of some kind, certainly not just prison. A lot of people could think that some Christians might have acquired a crisis 'foxhole faith' or a 'jailhouse religion' that did not last. Or perhaps they could think a life in Christ ensures that a Christian's life is insulated from ever having problems again."

"Honey," she continued, "do you remember the file cabinet full of letters we received from *Daddy* and all the people who were blessed by it? Many were from people serving time in prison. If we write the rest of our story, it will give such hope to those who are incarcerated to know they can not only make it through their sentence but have a life afterward."

Before I went to prison, we came to Christ within the same few minutes of each other, in separate cities, without the other knowing what each had done.

"Remember the drive home from Florida?" I said, "When I first told you about my God experience, you weren't very accepting."

"I simply wasn't there yet," she said. "But when it happened, boy, did it happen! It wasn't twenty-four hours after asking the Lord to take hold of my life that I felt on top of this world, in spite of the circumstances we faced. I continually found myself grinning from ear to ear and telling anybody who would listen about what I had recently done. I walked as though my feet were a foot off the ground. Then I would return to earth for a moment and realize my husband had been indicted. I knew nothing good was coming of that, but I had no fear. Both of us began devouring the Word. There was no comfort or satisfaction away from the Scriptures."

So we couldn't *not* write the rest of the story.

Even before I went to prison, Harvey and I went to church all over town. Sunday morning services at the Cathedral of St. Philip Episcopal Church, Sunday evening services at First Baptist Atlanta, Monday night back St. Philip's for prayer and praise, Wednesday nights at Mt. Paran Church of God, and on Thursdays we studied under independent Bible teacher Jim Tumlin. We wanted as much of Jesus Christ as we could incorporate into our lives. Harvey also went to several women's Bible studies at other churches in town.

We constantly discussed what we learned, compared notes, and sought answers to our questions from those wiser and more mature in Christ. Seeing the origins of God's plan of salvation in the Old Testament thrilled us. The Gospels just got more and more mind-boggling. Then the epistles taught us how we needed to live this new life in Christ.

We'd had ten months from the time we asked Jesus into our lives until I left for prison. The more we studied, the more faith we developed, and we realized that when people talk about having faith, they were often talking about faith in faith. But we quickly came to realize that faith must have an object, and the object of our faith was Jesus Christ.

When I first went to prison in 1979, the federal and state prison populations totaled about forty-eight thousand.

In 2014 the combined prison population stood at over 2.2 million. And tens of millions more are in personal prisons of their own making. People need to be encouraged to not only believe in God but to *believe* God.

We are more certain of our faith now after three-plus decades as believers than we were the first day in Christ because we've lived it. My wife and I did not fall away. We wouldn't change our journey for anything. And we're thrilled to share it with you.

*Chapter 22*

# PRISON IN MY REARVIEW MIRROR

*ome.* I had come home to my family. All the daydreams, prayers, and hopes came to fruition. After eighteen months at Eglin Prison Camp, I was where I belonged and wanted to be.

And being home, I needed a job. So I called Don Patterson, who was influential in leading Harvey and me to the faith. He invited me to lunch the next day to join him in the executive dining room at the Edwards Baking Company. I relished being served by a steward in black pants and a white jacket. Prison was right where it needed to be, in my rearview mirror.

Don asked pointed questions about my plans for the future.

"Right now, I really don't have any," I said. "And my résumé may very well disqualify me. But the terms of my release require me to have employment within the next thirty days. So if there is anything here that I could possibly do, I'd truly appreciate it." My spiritual life seemed to go from mountaintop experience to mountaintop experience in spite of my circumstances, and I half expected Don to say something like, "Would you consider being the head of marketing?" so I might have another "Praise the Lord" testimony.

He offered me a job, and I accepted. But it was not the head of marketing. In fact, I wasn't sure what he'd find for me to do until he called me later that afternoon.

The next morning I showed up at eight, properly attired in a T-shirt and work pants—the same Eglin Air Force Base hand-me-down navy blues I wore in prison. And Don introduced me to the maintenance crew. They were expanding their plant, which required a jackhammer to break up a concrete floor and us to throw the chunks into a truck. I would have liked a pair of steel-toe shoes as I risked having my foot smashed through my thin basketball shoes. That said, it was so good to be home and financially contributing that I was probably the most grateful person who was nearly vibrated to death.

I hoped to soon be finished with throwing concrete and get involved inside on the business side of baking, and I remained at Edwards until my old back problems that had confronted me in prison started to resurface after only nine weeks. I also had a second reason to leave. The break room had freshly brewed coffee and every delicious pie known to modern man. What else would a baking company have in the break room? I was becoming addicted to sugar and those pies were my fix.

Blake also needed to see my prison time in his own rearview mirror. I soon realized how difficult my time away had been for him. Suddenly he had a father who corrected him, whereas before he regarded Harvey as his sole authority figure. Now there was someone else competing for time with his mother; he had to share her with me.

Blake's first-grade teacher, whom I'll call Mrs. Bradshaw, sent home a note: "Blake is not doing well in school." She set up a meeting with Harvey and me. Mrs. Bradshaw told us that Blake's grades were suffering because of his bad behavior. She concluded that he acted out his frustrations and problems by attempting to attract attention. He did get the attention he wanted, only it was negative attention.

A few minutes into the meeting, she called Blake into the room. She gave him her most professional smile and paused. "Your parents and I have had a discussion about you, your work, and the fact that you have continued to be disruptive in the classroom."

Blake dropped his gaze. He was seated between Harvey and me, with Mrs. Bradshaw across the desk in front of us. I sensed his apprehension and put a hand on his shoulder, but he didn't look up.

As Mrs. Bradshaw talked on and described his behavior, Blake cautiously glanced at her, then at his mother. Finally he dropped his head, obviously ashamed and defeated. Then Mrs. Bradshaw began to question him, citing the wrongs he had committed and asking him in each case, "Is that true, Blake?" or something to that effect. I could see what she was trying to do—get him to acknowledge what he had done—but it began to feel like a criminal hearing. After a while, just as Blake began to cry, I had to interrupt.

"Mrs. Bradshaw, I hope you don't mind, but I have something to say."

"Certainly, Mr. Lawson." She smiled appreciatively.

"As you know, Mrs. Bradshaw, I made mistakes when I was operating my real estate investment firm. You're aware that I spent eighteen months in prison. Because of all the events that led up to that tragedy, I became a Christian. I received God's forgiveness because he loved me in spite of the poor choices I had made."

Mrs. Bradshaw appeared to be uncomfortable with my talk about prison. She tried to interrupt, but I tightened my grip on Blake's shoulder and continued. Blake had stopped crying and was looking at me.

"Blake had to learn early in life that even daddies make mistakes. That's a hard lesson for a boy so young to learn. Knowing God's forgiveness has totally changed my life. But frankly, if Blake hadn't forgiven me I don't know if I could have lived. When he was five years old, he forgave me for all the wrong things I had done and for abandoning him by going to prison. He forgave me for the shame I brought to him. I know he suffered the taunts of other children because of where I was.

He forgave me when I couldn't be with him for the Father-and-Son Day here at school. I couldn't be with him on his birthday and Christmas. He visited me in prison—out of love. I didn't deserve the kind of loyalty Blake gave to me. He loved me when I least deserved it."

I turned to Blake, and choking back emotion, said, "I'm trying to say that I love you, son. Just as you forgive me for all the wrong things I've done, I forgive you for everything you've done up to this moment. The slate is wiped clean."

I couldn't say anymore. I glanced at Harvey, and her smile confirmed that I had done the right thing. I hadn't spoken loudly or in anger. The words had come out softly because they were a mixture of joy and pain.

To her credit, Mrs. Bradshaw sat in silence. The professionalism vanished, and her eyes told me that she had witnessed something unusual—forgiveness taking place. I'm sure she didn't have these kinds of parent-teacher conferences on a regular basis.

Dear Harvey broke the silence by turning to Blake. "Is there anything you would like to tell Mrs. Bradshaw?"

He nodded and took a deep breath. "I'm sorry, Mrs. Bradshaw. I'm really sorry. I promise to be a better boy. Will you . . . forgive me?"

"Oh, yes, Blake. Yes! And . . . will you forgive me too? I realize that I haven't been as nice toward you as I could have been. I'm sorry too."

"Oh, that's okay."

We all laughed nervously, not sure how to exit from such an intense few moments.

"Blake, your dad mentioned that daddies make mistakes," Mrs. Bradshaw said, her eyes glistening. "I have to be honest enough to say that teachers make mistakes as well."

As we left the building, Blake ran out the door and took a short cut across the wet lawn to reach the car first. Harvey and I watched him while we followed, hand-in-hand. He stood at the door, beaming at us.

In that moment I wanted to say a hundred things to my son. He had shown such maturity and compassion in the past eighteen months. I gave him a hug. "Come on, son, let's all go for a milkshake!"

*Chapter 23*

# MOVING UP

Prior to my release from Eglin, Chuck Colson had offered me the position of director for the State of Georgia with Prison Fellowship, but I told him I wasn't at all sure that a career in Christian ministry was a natural fit. We talked further, and I expressed that even in my considering the position, my motives weren't pure. I knew it was something I could do well. The job description was to be visible in the community by sharing my testimony and the value of church involvement in prison ministries with the assistance of Prison Fellowship which stood ready to assist churches. The other aspect of the position was to train volunteers and equip them for the difficult task of going into the local prisons to be the Lord's representative. The state director needed to be a combination of Billy Graham and General Patton. My impure motive was that I felt the position would look good on my résumé for future employment. With Chuck's understanding, we agreed I should accept the position and leave the rest to the Lord's direction.

My first responsibility was to find a sweetheart deal

on an office rental—like free! The second was to meet all the Atlanta prison volunteers already in place who had been faithfully going into Georgia's prisons week after week, year after year. They were dedicated people who immediately earned my trust and respect. Through them I met lifers who had given their lives to Christ and although behind bars were finally free of the chains that had bound them all their lives.

Some people have said, "But when a person is in dire circumstances, don't you think it's possible they invent something like a loving and forgiving God for themselves just to put one foot in front of the other?" As if this is what changed those prisoner's lives—and mine.

Sadly, my family and old friends were the least likely to respond to the gospel. The truth is they need God just as badly as the people in prison and must also become the object of prayer because only the Holy Spirit can break through these barriers.

The thing I learned was, after the breakthroughs, people with great testimonies also need to mature and be supported through the long run.

One day Margaret Ann called Harvey and me to report that her home had been robbed. The perpetrator had been caught and was taken to the DeKalb County jail. Margaret Ann asked if I could arrange for us to visit this guy, Johnny, because she wanted to tell him he was forgiven and to explain that Jesus loves him. The next day we went and were led to a small room with two metal chairs. Thick plexiglass separated us from the prisoners. A guard opened a door on the opposite side, and a young, sheepish fellow in his twenties came and sat down in his chair. He hadn't the slightest idea what was going on other than the person whose house he broke into wanted to talk with him. Margaret Ann opened with some pictures her young children had drawn and sent with her as a gift. As she started, she began to tear up, then cry and sob. "S-S-teve, y-you talk to him, p-p-please."

Johnny sat impassively. We talked for a while, and Johnny followed me in prayer to ask Christ into his life. After his release his life seemed to change, and Margaret Ann gave of herself unselfishly and spent a considerable amount of time mentoring the young man. She and he had many church speaking engagements together. Prison Fellowship featured him in one of their monthly mailings, and Johnny became an overnight celebrity—one of those great coming-to-Christ stories we read about. But it wasn't long before he became less and less available. Finally, there was no contact. Johnny fell away.

I am now of the opinion that all new Christians should be silent for at least a year before they are permitted to share their witness—no matter if their name is Johnny or Steve Lawson. Dangerous stuff, being a Christian witness! I suppose that's one reason the Lord kept Paul sequestered for such a long period. The passage of time gives authority to the message. Now, so many years later, I look at this time of evangelism with mixed feelings. I know I brought the message of Jesus Christ to many. Based on my availability, I have no idea what the Holy Spirit accomplished. However, I regret at times I used the Lord's gift of electrifying speech to preach a great salvation message without an equally heavy a call to sanctification and holy living. If I had done more of that, perhaps some would not have fallen away.

My immediate supervisor at Prison Fellowship was also a prison alumnus. He was regional director for three states in the Southeast, including Georgia. He had been the go-to person in each state. He truly loved the Lord and his position with Prison Fellowship. The contacts he had coordinated for many years readily accepted me, and it was an easy transfer of responsibilities.

Within a year, however, I was working under a new regional director whose style was to micromanage. Soon it became an untenable situation for both of us, and he terminated my employment, something that hadn't happened to me since high school when I worked in giftwrap during one Christmas season at a department store in Manhattan. I felt humiliated and hollowed out. Chuck Colson had personally asked me to be state director, and here I was fired. Although I left on good terms with the ministry, and Chuck Colson would write the foreword in *Daddy* years later, the Friday morning prayer group really didn't understand what had happened.

I felt a current of pride raise its ugly head. I felt injured. If a person did well, it meant the Lord was honoring his life—as I, and many others, assumed. If not, he wasn't. Ministries are always measured against the numbers to validate their mission and their existence. So many of us have become "blessing junkies" and validate individual lives the same way. To me, it seems like a shallow gospel with the Evil One's fingerprints all over it. But it's amazing how many people buy into it. Even after being in the faith for many years, sometimes it takes effort to keep one's eyes on the faith rather than the faithful. All that aside, Harvey and I saw the larger truth of the Lord's having other plans for my life. I couldn't dwell on it for long because I needed to be employed—so back to looking for a job.

*Chapter 24*

# MOVING DOWN

R andy Bevins was a member of my prayer group at the Cathedral of St. Philip, and he suggested we have an early breakfast on Saturday morning. Randy was an astute real estate investor and owned parking lots throughout the Southeast. While I was at Eglin we had corresponded, and even back then, he'd suggested that when I returned home he'd be happy to talk to me about a position with his firm. Most would assume he made his exceptional living by parking fees. What most didn't consider was that the parking fees also paid the mortgage on the land until he was able to sell at much higher prices. His wealth in this now-large firm came more from real estate than parking itself. I saw many possibilities where I could be a good fit, such as property sales, land acquisition, management, public relations, or human resources. Perhaps he was looking to delegate a good amount of responsibility to have time for other pursuits.

"There could be a lot of people who would have a problem with your past incarceration, honey," Harvey said.

"But I don't think another strong Christian would. If he's looking for an executive talent, you'd be the best hire he could make."

Randy was on the church vestry and often spoke to the congregation about giving back to the Lord through tithes and offerings. He was a member of Companies for Christ, whose members did things to bring Jesus Christ into their business and to the community. Edwards Baking Company, for example, embossed Scripture verses in each pie tin. I looked forward to whatever opportunity Randy would present me.

We met for breakfast, and I explained the situation surrounding my previous job. "I don't think a career in full-time ministry is what God has in mind for me," I said. "That's why I was so enthused about our meeting. I have no qualms about being part of another's team. Nor am I concerned about compensation. I know you'll be more than fair. The only goal I have is to do the job well and to earn your confidence. Tell me, where do you see my talents being best used?"

Randy's eyebrows arched a bit and he looked desperately uncomfortable.

"Steve, I'm afraid there's a misunderstanding." He paused. "You're a talented and gifted guy, and there isn't any position within my firm, including mine, where you wouldn't be overqualified. But the spot I can make available for you is at our Georgia State University location. The manager there is relocating, so the position is open. The hours are from six in the morning until two in the afternoon. Your job will be to dispense tickets, take the money, and tidy up the parking area. The only other responsibility you'll have is to manage time cards and to shore up any shortfall when people don't show up. We're not talking about the most dependable of employees, I'm afraid. They often pick up their checks and drink them away. Our firm gets a subsidy from the government for each hire because we offer employment to individuals who might otherwise not be able to find work."

I steadied myself with a hand on the table and breathed through my mouth to regulate my spiking heart rate. "Well, you're right, Randy," I said in recovery from shock. "Right now any income I'm able to bring into the house will be welcomed. When do I start, and what's the salary?"

My, how far I had fallen.

"If you're able to begin Monday, that will work perfectly for us, Steve. The manager's salary is one dollar and twenty-five cents an hour above the minimum wage, and we pay everyone each Friday.

One dollar and twenty-five cents above minimum wage. Oh boy.

"Louie is the guy who's leaving, and he'll show you the ropes." Randy paid and said, "Steve, you look great. Good to have you on board even though I know it won't be for long. Guys like you don't let any grass grow under their feet. You wear a large shirt, don't you? I'll have a clean company logo shirt waiting for you."

"Good to be part of the team, Randy. I'll see Louie Monday morning at six."

I returned home and told Harvey.

"Oh, Stephen, How demoralizing! You must have been devastated. I'm amazed you were able to handle it. Oh my word I am afraid of what I could have said in the moment. My Christian witness could have vanished in a fit of temper. Were we wrong to envision something more? Lord, please help Stephen and me see our way through this. Right now I can't even think clearly."

We knew we had to pray for Randy and thank God for the job opportunity at that moment. But Harvey was still mad. We practiced releasing our disappointment and anger to God and asked him to give us the necessary forgiveness to go forward.

"Honey," I said, "it'll never go down as one of my Kodak moments. But I can't sit around the house like an executive while you're out there busting your chops. I've got to be employed and bring something in. I don't know when the Lord will choose to restore us, but when he does, he'll find me busy. Remember when you were in show business? There was an old saying, 'There are no bit parts, only bit actors.' "

"What does that have to do with anything?"

"No honest job should be beneath my dignity. Patience has never been one of my strong virtues, but I don't see any other options right now. While I was in prison Blake often mentioned how hard you worked and asked if I'd help you earn money when I got home because you were so tired from working so hard. I'm so happy to be home with you and Blake and thrilled to be working that no disappointment can overwhelm my joy. I have the most wonderful feeling when he sees me go to work and come home."

Harvey and I learned that praying for someone who offended you or caused you pain removes the sting of the event. Continuing to dislike someone you are praying for is truly difficult. The more you pray for someone, the more you see what God sees about them. Randy never meant it for harm. He offered what he had, so to God be the glory! We survived and could joke later about my being the best parking lot attendant in Atlanta.

With time in the afternoon and weekends available, I augmented my income through a part-time job with a company that moved business offices to new locations. Five or six times I helped relocate firms whose employees I used to socialize with. Some of my new blue-collar buddies did the heavy lifting, and some rolled the desks and filing cabinets on dollies. I was a "roller"! Did I find this to be a humbling experience? Frankly, no. My days were long but gratifying though not particularly stimulating. I knew that if I was faithful in smaller things, the Lord would allow me to be faithful in larger things. I didn't know how or when it would happen, but I was sure it would. In the meantime, I chose to do my current jobs with a grateful spirit and a joyful heart. I was mindful of the Scripture that said the Lord loved the cheerful giver—not merely one who gave.

# Chapter 25

# HIDDEN DANGER

It was a Wednesday evening. We had finished dinner, and Blake, Harvey, and I were huddled on the sofa watching one of Blake's favorite television programs. The phone rang from the other room. Harvey got up and answered it.

"Yes, he's here. May I tell him who's calling? Sure, Dave, let me get him for you."

I gave her an unknowing expression and walked to the phone.

"Steve, it's Dave Bingham*," he said. "How are you doing?" Dave was a nice guy and had a good intellect, something not plentiful in the Florida zip code where the prison was located. During my time at Eglin Prison Camp we spent time together in conversations and playing tennis. Dave was good company and had done time for a drug-related incident. In prison, if a person wants to go into detail about his crime, he'll freely bring it up. If he doesn't, it's never wise to ask. It's never a good idea to have anyone assume you're too interested. It's never a good idea for another inmate to wonder if a person is a government plant or an inmate snitch attempting to lessen one's sentence with useful information.

"Hello, Dave. What a nice surprise. What are you up to?" It really was a surprise. I was still on probation, which meant my probation officer would show up at unannounced times to check on me. I need his permission to travel outside of Atlanta, and one of the major rules was that I was to have no contact with any ex-felon. If it ever happened, I was to contact my parole officer immediately. We made small talk for about five minutes. The entire time, I wondered what the call was all about, because although we were friendly at Eglin, we were far from friends. When I left, I never imagined I'd ever hear his name again.

"How's the money situation on your end, Steve," he said. "If you're a little low on funds I might be a blessing to you. I've got something that needs to be done with someone I really feel is a guy I'm able to trust, and the money's good."

"Sure, money's tight, Dave. What do you have in mind?"

"On Friday, there will be a black Ford parked in the Lenox Square Shopping Center by Neiman Marcus. I can give you the tag number by tomorrow. The car will be locked, but the key will be on top of the front tire on the passenger side. All I need is for you to drive the car to the Raleigh-Durham Airport, leave it there, and put the key back where you found it. In the car you'll find a one-way ticket back to Atlanta. Do you think $10,000 would help right about now?"

"Of course! I can't remember a time in my life an extra $10,000 in cash wouldn't help," I said with humor. Dave, I don't want to ask any questions, and I know you don't want to answer any, but I just have a feeling it's something

I shouldn't do. I appreciate your calling and thinking of me, though."

"Come on, Steve. This will take no time at all, and I don't know anyone in Atlanta other than you. Help a guy out, won't you?" I was off the phone within the next minute. The answer was still no. After we had put Blake to bed, we went to the kitchen in order to finish loading the dishwasher and cleaning up.

"Who is Dave, and what was that about?" Harvey said. "You looked unsettled when you came back into the room with Blake and me." I told her of Dave's request, and Harvey asked if I planned to speak to my probation officer about it.

"Frankly, I'd just as soon forget he ever called. What he may be doing or not doing is really none of my business; and in prison, ratting someone out is really bad business," I said. "Aside from that, we only have suspicion to go on. I don't know anything for a fact."

"Honey, you're sounding like every attorney we've ever known. They always claim to have never known anything and that we just assumed they did. That's always the escape hatch. But your contract with the probation department is to report any contact from an ex-felon. On that basis alone, you have to notify them. But let me ask you something else. Suppose Dave was caught doing something and is working with the government on a plea bargain, and suppose part of it is to be a one-man sting operation to catch someone in his net?"

My eyes widened. There was no response other than to acknowledge the truth of her discernment—which seemed to be confirmed when I called my probation officer the next day. He received the news with little response in the most understated and seemingly uninterested way, as though I had given him a halftime hockey score from Bulgaria.

Both opportunity and danger can come without expectation. Discerning the variance can spell the difference between a life of blessing and a life of suffering—especially for an ex-con. The path of redemption is full of danger.

Through the work of God I had been released after only eighteen months. But if Dave's offer had been real, and I was caught—or if as we suspect, it had been a sting, and I went along—I would have gone back to prison for the full eight-year sentence. Even Harvey could have been indicted and imprisoned just for answering the phone. That one phone call was so dangerous it made us shudder.

# Chapter 26

# BRANDED

"Two years, Harvey! I'm amazed I've been out of prison that long already."

With Blake at a friend's house, we had the night to ourselves to celebrate with grilled steak and wine. But things weren't like they used to be. "Our social life is certainly more subdued than it was once upon a time."

"Well, Stephen! Are you just now noticing we live a very quiet lifestyle? Honey, it's been this way ever since you left for prison and probably won't change anytime soon."

What I had been pondering for some time was so obvious to Harvey.

"Honey," she said, "Once you left, Blake and I were the objects of ministry. In one way, people were absolutely wonderful, and I don't know what we would have done without the Lord working through so many. On the other hand, I found that some folks didn't want to get too close because they were afraid they would be confronted with any additional needs we had and didn't want to be put in an uncomfortable position."

She gently reminded me that since Blake had always attended private school, and besides paying for the top-notch education, parents also look for the future networking it provides for the kids. So they throw lavish birthday parties. They go on skiing vacations together. They try to go to the same vacation spots in the summer, or they hang out at the club together. All of these things cost a lot of money, and we did those things like everyone else when we were financially able. But now we were excluded because we couldn't afford to be included.

As she went on, the reasoning became clear. We used to go to any restaurant or event with another couple and not care who picked up the tab—or didn't—because all of us had plenty of money. If we didn't pick up the check this time we would the next. No one wanted to go out to dinner with us now because they didn't want to place us in an uncomfortable financial position. They weren't staying away because they're unkind. They were sparing us the awkward situation of our having to decline an invitation because we could not afford the evening out.

"I'd better have another glass of wine," I said.

She said she understood life so much better now. She recognized that friendships are generally reciprocal; business and social relationships are beneficial and advantageous to each party, and there's nothing wrong with that as long as you don't put too much stock in it. Deals can be made on the golf course or at a dinner party just as well as in an office. You're great as long as you're able to say yes or write a check to the charity du jour. Your reputation increases if you can offer your lovely home for a fundraiser. But when things turn bad or, God forbid, you go to prison, those same people who thought you were terrific might now say, "I suspected all along he cut corners," or "I never bought him for a minute." She accepted that it was all part of the human condition.

"Okay, but that was our life before Christ," I said. "We're talking about Christians here. I can't tell you how many people I've met since coming home who were startled to meet me and said, 'I've been praying for you for several years.' And every time I speak somewhere, people are thrilled to hear our testimony, and they are so warm and eager to meet us."

So she enlightened me further, "People are people—Christian or not." When you left, it took me a long time to feel comfortable being out in public for concern of running into old friends or investors. It took a lot of prayer, and the only option I had was to believe *God's* opinion of us." Through prayer she released people's opinions whether real or something she imagined, to the Lord. My being in prison was bad enough, but she got to a point where she would no longer allow herself to feel destroyed by people who by their looks or gossip would make her a prisoner as well. She had to work through those issues on her own, and she just couldn't burden me with what someone said or the times she felt a cold shoulder from someone at Blake's school or even at church. "I overcame it through the grace of God," she said. "But I didn't like it." Even at church a person here or there would point and whisper, "Oh, there she is. Her husband's in prison." She even overheard it in the ladies' room and had to walk out. She learned to accept that it just came with the territory.

"Oh, Lord. I hadn't plumbed the depths of all this before," I said. The best I could do was cling to Romans 8:1–2: "Therefore, there is now no condemnation for those who are in Christ Jesus, because through Christ Jesus the law of the Spirit who gives life has set you free from the law of sin and death."

Those eighteen months I was gone were lonely for her. Invitations to lunch or dinner were scarce. And they still were. Yet she realized now that this is right where the Lord wanted her, and if this is part of the cost to know Christ, she was happy to stay right where we were. This helped me understand the reason people weren't falling over themselves to offer me career positions. Besides that, Christians can be like any other folks. They don't want to hear bad news.

I thought about it and realized that when we were invited somewhere, it almost seemed that I was there for a personal Q&A session. I wondered if we were invited because we were an object of ministry and a onetime experience. It seemed that way. Come to think of it, everyone seemed to be fascinated to know someone with a prison experience.

In looking through the letters I received when *Daddy* was published, many asked how long it took for me to consider myself an ex-felon or if I was always expected to wear a scarlet letter on my chest, maybe *C* for criminal or *S* for sinner. I wasn't able to answer the question back then but certainly am able to now.

All these years later, I'm able to recall all of the events of my past, but they no longer hold the sting they once did. On one hand, it's a stretch to think that I ever woke up and went to sleep in a federal prison. It's hard to believe there was ever a time in my life I placed a bet. I've been forgiven, first by God, second by Harvey and Blake, then by myself. When we repent and ask forgiveness, God forgives and is faithful to remember no more. On the other hand, we remember our sins for two reasons: first, so we don't go there again, and second, so that we are credible to others going through a similar experience. It's hard for me to minister to someone who has experienced sexual abuse. Yet others are quite effective in that area because of their own past.

I knew I was progressing when I no longer made lengthy explanations. Most prison alumni give long answers in effort to leave no doubt their answers are honest ones. We struggle with feelings about the past and want to close the credibility gap.

Yet some people—almost like God—have surprisingly little concern or remembrance that I or anyone else was in prison. While walking through a department store, Harvey and I ran into an old friend. It had been ages since we last talked. As the conversation progressed, I mentioned that I hadn't seen this person since I'd returned from prison. She looked at me with a strange expression. "Oh, Steve, I hadn't remembered you ever went to prison."

That's God's approach. "As far as the east is from the west, so far has he removed our transgressions from us. As a father has compassion on his children, so the LORD has compassion of those who fear him" (Psalm 103:12–13).

# Chapter 27

# ANOTHER CHANCE

I f you were producing a movie and needed a person who looked like a distinguished president of a Fortune 500 company or the Bishop of a church, Central Casting would send A. Anderson Huber. Andy was a well-intentioned guy, who's since gone to be with the Lord. He was about five feet nine inches tall with a beautiful prematurely grey head of hair and a ruddy complexion. At the time, he was a vice president with Bank of America, and although his suite of offices was a block away, he had an unobstructed view of my parking lot.

It was March, with temperatures in the forties under the sunlight of an exceptionally clear day. The morning traffic had come and parked, so I picked up the litter on the deck, a task made easier by a wind that herded most of the trash into the cement corner of the property. I pulled the chair from my small hut, sat in the sun, and tilted back against the wall. The phone rang.

"Parking lot sixteen," I said.

"Mr. Lawson, this is Mr. Huber's office calling." I recognized his administrator's voice. "Are you available to take his call?"

"Yes, I just finished a director's meeting, and my schedule looks pretty clear for the next fifteen minutes." She chuckled and put me through to Andy.

"You seem to be enjoying yourself sunbathing down there," he said in his clipped Ivy League accent. The rest of us just aren't that fortunate."

"Andy, you've got to slow down and take time to smell the roses. Why don't you take off that jacket and tie, roll up your sleeves, and join me out here for a few rays? It'll do you the world of good."

"So how are things going in the fast lane of the parking business?"

"Nothing out of the ordinary, Andy, but I do appreciate your asking," I said.

"Steve, I'd like you to call Richard Kessler, the CEO at Days Inn of America. He'd like to meet with you and assured me he will find something for you over there in the corporate offices. I've already gone over your background with him."

Just then I felt as if time stopped, as if the whole world stopped, just for me. My hard road of redemption found space for a breakthrough blessing that left me at a loss for words. The most intelligent thing I could say was, "Does this mean that I have to give up parking?"

"Yes, and you'll have to limit your sunbathing to weekends."

"Andy, that's great! I can't thank you enough. We're talking about a job inside a building, right? A place where a guy wears a suit and tie?"

"You'll have to go over the dress codes with him, my friend. But prior to your interview I'd take off that chocolate brown shirt with the company logo in favor of something more respectable looking."

"You have good eyesight."

"I'm looking at you through binoculars."

# Chapter 28

# DAYS INN–AND OUT

D ays Inn is a budget-priced motel company founded by Cecil Day, who died of cancer early in his life, and his wife now owned the majority of the stock. She ran the Cecil B. Day Foundation while chief executives ran the motel business. The company was thirteen years old, and each quarter exceeded profit records attained the preceding quarter. After a fifteen-minute interview, human resources assigned me to the marketing department. My salary was $400 a week. I thought I had died and gone to heaven. This was especially true when I looked out the window from my desk to see it pouring rain.

Harvey was as excited as I was. "Oh, honey, I'm so thrilled for you. God has heard our prayers and he hasn't forgotten us."

I agreed. And in short order two things became apparent. The first was how young everyone was. For the most part I was many years senior to nearly everyone else. The second was the entrepreneurial mindset of the marketing department. Those who developed a personal marketing strategy received promotions and bonuses. Ideas seemed to bounce off every wall. Some offered an idea of having airport propertie⁻ turn their rooftops into billboards that airline passengers would note as they took off or landed. Another, who didn't stay long, suggested a rooftop sign that was to say "Love Thy Neighbor—HERE!"

After three months, I explained a marketing concept idea with my VP of marketing, and he gave me the green light and budget to see if I could make it happen.

I drove around the southeastern states and visited every known small-college athletic association. "So, basically, Mr. Commissioner, the bottom-line goal for us is to have all the men's and women's athletic teams in your conference stay at Days Inn when traveling to play other schools. We'll offer attractive personal rates too. I'll even make your conference a charter member of our Varsity Club of America. Our understanding is that most of the athletic conferences and schools with larger budgets really don't fit our profile. Let's face it, the income-producing sports, like basketball and football, tend to stay at Hilton or Marriott hotels. I'll bet you don't have many of those properties beating your doors down with special offers."

"None, really," he said.

"Exactly. Days Inn will use its cache to coordinate your conference and all the others in the Southeast through its Varsity Club of America. We'll establish joint purchasing power that will have these same vendors give us the same prices as the larger colleges. There's no cost to you. All I need is a letter saying you fundamentally endorse the idea and look forward to reviewing the complete business plan and contracts when they are available."

The concept grabbed a foothold. Days Inn would receive an upsurge in room rentals and a commission or finder's fee from vendors' sales of athletic supplies. I did not receive one negative response. I spent the following three months making myself visible with these commissioners and other interested parties.

But in business, no matter who you are or how good you are or how hard you work, not all things are fair. Sometimes we gain, and sometimes we lose.

Weekly rumors and gossip often made their way up and down the office hallways. The latest was that our senior vice president of marketing was leaving the firm, although no one seemed to know who was initiating the action. In this case, the rumors held true. A new head of marketing was arranging his corner office almost before the other had left the building. The new broom swept clean, and more than half the marketing department was terminated with a month's salary. I was one of them—despite all my rising success.

I requested Days Inn release my Varsity Club of America concept to me. They declined.

# Chapter 29

# LIGHT AT ROCK BOTTOM

For the first time since becoming a Christian, I felt utterly defeated. Worse than I ever felt when going to prison. Where was God in all this? "We can't go on this way," I said to Harvey. "God says he will never allow more than we can endure, but I wish he'd consult with me because I am quickly reaching my maximum limit!"

I collected unemployment. I looked for jobs without success. Where was this God who was so concerned about me and loved me? The one who called on the hounds of heaven to track me down seemed totally unconcerned about our struggles now. *How is God honored by my not being able to make a living? Am I toxic? Is God capricious? How am I supposed to speak of my conversion when I am starting to feel like a fraud? Why am I seeking a publisher for the book I wrote to share his faithfulness, which I now doubt?* I was so low I couldn't see the tops of my shoes. For the first time Harvey was negatively affected too. While all this was happening, we kept an upbeat demeanor around Blake, and he was a helpful diversion in directing our thoughts away from the pit we were in. On the other hand, he was a reminder of how far my being a failure stretched. I was unable to pray and couldn't have cared less about trying. And save the positive confessions for someone else. Name it and claim it—a joke. Blab it and grab it—just as dumb. What kind of witness is it for a Christian unable to hold employment or pay his bills?

Then Harvey asked me a question for which I had no answer. "Stephen, looking at what we're going through, what does it have to do with the virgin birth of Christ, his death, and his resurrection? I mean, how can our feelings and situation invalidate what we know to be true? I feel exactly the same way you do, and my emotions are on a rollercoaster just like yours. We're mad as we can be at God, but in a strange way, it is a display of faith. It is an admission that he alone is in control. He is God and Lord of all."

I called our friend and the priest at St. Patrick's Episcopal Church, Gray Temple, and set up an appointment and told him I needed prayer. I have always had a deep respect for Gray and appreciated his insight and prayer, but frankly I didn't think I felt one bit better as I left his office. Yet I awoke the next morning sensing something was different. The cloud of despair seemed to be lifted, and I realized I was tired of being depressed—just sick of being sick. I certainly wasn't without knowledge of the truth and knew exactly where to go in Scripture to allow the Lord to minister to me. It seemed as if the Evil One had come along and tried to imprison me with a spirit of hopelessness, but Gray's prayers the day before had unlocked the cage door of my desolation, released and restored me to a right relationship with the Lord.

As I look back over the landscape of my life these past thirty-four years, I have the following advice to those currently reading this book: Devote your time to reading God's Word. When you become a Christian, it doesn't mean you become healthy, wealthy, and problem free. You're going to have trials just like every other living soul does. You don't go from mountaintop to mountaintop experience. You remain in a battlefield for your soul. It is warfare conducted by the spirits of darkness and of principalities. The Evil One hates your becoming a Christian in the first place, but he hates an effective Christian even more, where the testimony of God's strength is perfected in your weakness, where his life lived through you has the power to change lives. But Harvey was right. What do our personal problems have to do with the reality of Jesus Christ?

We see more clearly now than we did at the time. It isn't that people didn't want to be of assistance to us, they just wanted to observe our walk and attitude for a generous period before they came to the judgment of our being "gold" as opposed to "fool's gold."

Here's another truth, and there isn't a Christian this hasn't happened to early in their Christian walk: Christians have often allowed emotion to overtake spiritual judgment. We all have our personal stories of being burned by not exercising our God-given discernment. Harvey and I once heard on television about some folks from England stranded at the Greyhound bus terminal because someone had stolen their passports and money. We drove downtown and picked them up, and they lived in our home for several days before the consulate informed us they were con artists.

We know of someone else, a lovely Christian woman, who fell for another's sob story and befriended them only to learn the person was using her car to make drug deals. Other Christians have rushed in to assist when they were far ahead of the Lord for one reason or another, which could have been avoided through prayer and seeking confirmation from other Christians or their pastor.

Seeing from this viewpoint lifted my spirits. And things started improving from there.

# Chapter 30

# FINALLY FLYING

I've learned to recognize when the Lord has truly spoken through Harvey because the words seem to cascade out of her mouth and are as strong as an acre of garlic. It was during this time that Harvey said she felt the Lord's peace over our direction.

"I came to believe that Stephen would never hold meaningful employment if we were to depend on others to make it happen. Even when an opportunity existed, one never knew when the corporate winds would change and you'd find yourself in that figurative parking lot on the outside looking in. We needed to be in business for ourselves."

After several stops and starts my attention was called to the travel agency business. I was aware how an agency operates because Days Inn had a travel office in the Day building for their business travelers, and a local travel agency provided the travel agents. I knew I couldn't sell a product where I had to convince someone on the merits of my product—much less an investment. You can't make a sale when everyone knows you need to make it to survive.

The travel agency business seemed to have everything I was looking for. It is a service-related industry. There's no inventory. The airline pays you to sell their seats, and the service you provide is free to the customer. It's a straightforward business, and experienced travel agents are always available. I didn't have to convince a business in Atlanta to send someone to Detroit—they were going there anyway. What could be more generic than an airline seat? Further, the airline automation systems are on lease from the airlines. The retail space you operate out of is leased, and the furniture you furnish it with is inexpensive. In a perfect world, everything should fit in to your cash flow. The cash down stroke to get in business should be pretty minimal. The fundamental problem is that I didn't have the minimal!

I wrote a business and marketing plan. I would work as the outside salesman and bring in clients. Harvey would manage the inside. Neither of us knew anything about the travel agency business but knew we had the people skills and management skills to make a go of it. We found someone to financially underwrite the firm and provide us with a salary. This sounds a great deal easier than it was, but over time, God made provision for us. Ultimately Harvey left her job at the bank, and we worked together. We experienced a steady growth. One of our first clients was A. Anderson Huber at Bank of America. Our friend Victor Oliver introduced us to a number of Christian ministries that traveled internationally, and we began our business with a small client base of evangelical organizations and churches that had strong mission-sending programs.

Over years we acquired other agencies and merged them into our company. Although we handled corporate and vacation travel too, the heart and soul of our business was evangelical churches, Christian ministries, and mission-sending organizations.

After high school and before college, Blake spent a year with the ministry of Youth With A Mission (YWAM), attending a Discipleship Training School (DTS). He did a DTS and then a School of Evangelism (SOE) that together encompassed a year. This connection eventually led to our being asked to open an office in Kona, Hawaii, to handle the YWAM account, and our travel office was on the main campus. To this day our firm still handles the travel for Loren Cunningham, one of the founders of YWAM, and the travel of many other YWAM missionaries located around the world.

As years passed, our financial struggles lessened. However, Harvey would say, "You don't know anything about business until you experience making payroll on the fifteenth and last day of the month. Your employees must be paid, but the owner may have to wait many payroll periods before his or her salary can be justified." We could write another book on being a small business owner; and as much as we deeply appreciate those people who were partners with us in the early go, there is nothing like owning 100 percent of the business. Partners don't always see the mission and vision the same way you do. It doesn't make one right and the other wrong. We are just individuals, and fortunately God loves us corporately as Christians, but he also cares for us personally and will work with our individuality.

We have never lost sight of how far we have come, from working the parking lot to owning a successful business. God's love for each of us is more magnificent and profound than we can put into words.

As we pondered of how far we had come and what we learned from God in the process, we thought of major life lessons along the way, to where we'll now turn.

# Chapter 31

# LESSONS FROM PRISON

A s I mentioned in *Daddy*, I read Scripture for about two years after picking up a *Good News for Modern Man* Bible in Florida before asking Jesus into my life. Ten months after receiving Christ I was in the slammer. I knew then—but understand even more clearly after all these years—that there is a great difference between asking God to excuse your actions because of extenuating circumstances versus asking him to forgive you. Excuse comes with an appeal; repentance does not. God respects the latter, not the former. You can't manipulate God. Others much greater than you and I have tried without success. To the Lord, they must resemble a pigeon knocking over the pieces on a chessboard, then strutting around as if it won. A change of the heart changes the mind, and we no longer have a desire to sin. Now when we fall short of God's best or miss the mark, we want to make things right as soon as possible. You want out of that prison you've been in all your life? Keep short accounts with God.

The memory I shared in *Daddy* of saying good-bye to Blake and Harvey was one of the saddest days of my life. The Lord's pleasure wasn't that I should ever earn my way to prison. However, he promised that whatever the circumstances of my life, he would be in the fiery furnace with me. He promised that if I responded rightly, his truth would mold and conform me more to the image of his Son. In my prison experience, I learned for a fact that the Lord is true to his promise of never allowing more than I could bear. "No temptation has overtaken you except what is common to mankind. And God is faithful; he will not let you be tempted beyond what you can bear. But when you are tempted, he will also provide a way out so that you can endure it" (1 Corinthians 10:13). He always knew of my affliction and the troubles of my soul. He is just a prayer away from meeting with me. I sensed him holding me secure and not giving me over to the hand of the enemy. I learned he sets on high those who are lowly, and those who mourn, he lifts to safety. I know without a doubt that my Redeemer truly lives and that he never forsakes those who seek him. I have experienced his remaining faithful even when I am unfaithful. I know through experience his mercy endures forever. He rescued me (and continues to) because he delights in me. And he delights in me because I am his.

It's amazing the things you can convince yourself to do when you rationalize your behavior. As long as you are able to deceive yourself in the thought that your acts are justified, you are on the road to self-destruction. It's called situational ethics, and it demands your engagement in whatever deception is necessary to legitimize solving a problem. It need not be truthful, rational, or moral because the end always justifies the means. In most cases the person engaged in such an activity is the very last person to assume it pertains to them. They buy into the justifications long before the deceptions are out of the bag.

Mark this well: where ego, pride, and private sins exist, your personal demons will always win. I know for a fact that crisis surrounds the person who has not submitted his personal issues to Christ. Ungodly decisions are made because we return to the strongholds that continually keep us secure in our personal prison—and another has the key. We don't control those passions—they control us.

I learned in Christ that only godly motivations will get you to where you ultimately want to land. Otherwise, the payout always leaves you desiring more. Being financially successful allowed me to purchase all the things I thought I wanted. Little did I realize I had recreated the same performance-based situation as an adult that I had grown up with as a child. I hated it as a child and hated it no less as an adult. That is, perform up to here, and others will love and respect you at the same level. Those of us who have been trained this way will give testimony to the truth that the bar keeps being raised, and you never reach it. However, now that you're an adult, you think you control the level of the bar, but you don't. It means making more money or doing more, always more. And this lie is the enemy of a life at peace. When your success is the only thing that provides you with a feeling of validation, losing it is like a death. I always viewed myself through the eyes of what I assumed other people thought, and I aimed to match their successes.

In Christ I was able to give all that stuff up. It was only then a doomed life became one of value. At the end of our days a life of real value will not be measured by what you have accumulated in possessions or by your bank account. When the obituary gives notice of my death, I may well be the richest person on those pages, and so much of that richness comes from what I learned because of my time in prison.

# Chapter 32

# PRISON WISDOM

If you're in prison or about to go, realize that this bleak time of your life will pass. One day you will be released. Or if you're in for life with no parole or even on death row, even then you have a choice of how well you live the rest of your life. My hope is you will use your time productively. I've seen many go to prison and make contacts that will further their life in crime once they return home. In the alternative, why not take this opportunity to learn a skill or start or complete your college education? There are local colleges near your prison that will assist. Have you ever read the Bible cover to cover? That's a worthwhile project too. The first time I did, I was hoping to find errors so I could be in a position to put it down and never think of religion again. But if you say something like I did, "God, if you are really there, I'll read this, but the rest is up to you," that's an honest and often life-changing approach.

The reason most inmates leave the slammer as the same people they were when they entered is their continued inability to take total ownership of what they have done along with the reasons that motivated their actions. Most inmates assume their only problem centers on their incarceration, and once they get out, things will be different. But they are going to come out just like they went in because they have no roadmap or game plan to facilitate making a right and honest change in their thinking. Even if we exercise every bit of willpower we have, no one is good enough, smart enough, strong-willed or tough enough to make these changes by themselves and hope to make the change last. Take my word for it. I've tried. Does it take a shrink? Sometimes, maybe. Usually not. Just hard work—one-on-one with the Lord.

All my life I had arguments I thought were valid as to why God didn't exist or, if he did exist, how he was a cosmic being unaware or unconcerned about my life. If the first was true, why bother? If the second was true, again, why bother? I was a wellspring of knowledge when it came to theological discussions about abortion, euthanasia, and what a person needed to do to qualify for heaven. Imagine, if you will, a ladder from earth to heaven. Simple logic was that the rung I was standing on was a passing grade. Everything under me was a failing grade. The truth is I really didn't care and had no interest in pursuing it further because I made myself the final authority.

I found that many people in prison have a software problem. I was amazed to find that others went to prison for being jerks! Like me, they didn't have a criminal mentality but made wrong choices at the fork in the road, and their bad decisions caused them to earn their way to the slammer. Some may have heavy-duty psychological problems, but for the most part, they make rational decisions with understandable logic. Included in this group are people who seem totally rational but are anti any thought of religion and wouldn't pick up any book if they thought it had a spiritual bent. The chances of them reading this book, for example, are slim to none. For them, I have written a secular book, *Schmucks and Other White Collar Criminals*, with the subtitle *The Schmuck Stops Here*. People read it for laughs but find it to be a redemptive book that is intended to lead them to salvation. Currently, it's available for just ninety-nine cents at Amazon.com, and it has a huge market as, unfortunately, there are a lot of those folks out there.

I've often shared my conversion to Christ and explained that my story isn't as dramatic as someone who stopped drinking or gave up hard drugs. I didn't escape from a cult nor was I found abandoned as a child in a major city. However, after absorbing myself in reading Scripture, I took out a yellow legal pad and gave myself a forensic examination. On the left side, I wrote down incidents in my life I knew had to be major events along with a descriptive word or two to describe how each made me feel. One such event was when I was sent to Louisville to live with my mother's sister when I was fifteen years old. My descriptive word was *abandoned*. On the right side, I wrote how that emotion seemed to manifest itself in my life as an adult. I was shocked at the manifestation and how it seemed to direct my life. I refer to each as the root of the matter as opposed to the fruit of the matter.

Many people self-medicate problems. It's always done to relieve internal pain, and the self-medication varies from person to person. You may add to my list, but the more obvious are drinking, lying, gambling, and cheating. The outrageous things done are the fruits of the problem. For example, take drinking: a person drinks to excess, so people see that person's problem as being a drunkard. But a person drinks because of some other pain that is the true root of the problem. This is not to argue that alcohol abuse may also be an illness, but I suggest it began in order to cover a pain that a person was unable to identify or otherwise come to terms with.

If a person is known to lie, the root of the problem may be an overwhelming need to please and be found pleasing. A person with those needs will tell you what you want to hear, not tell you the truth. They puff and cloud the truth to receive praise or recognition. That's the fruit of the problem. The root of it may be deep-rooted feelings of inferiority and worthlessness. The risk taker can fall into gambling for a number or reasons, and the addicted gambler will bet on anything available. That's the fruit of the problem but more probable is the issue of depression, and the gambler has found that the serotonin levels in the brain can rise and give the participant a euphoric feeling when engaged in gambling. Just as a drug user continues to use, so the gambler will continue gambling while seeking euphoric feelings to ease the internal pain. Last is the person who cheats. It is the most secretive of the problems discussed and can incorporate all of the above mentioned problems. Those individuals will lie, cheat, drink and gamble away a marriage and family while allowing the activity to eat away at their soul. For some, any of the above activities can lead a person to prison. Others may seem to manage their lives better, but they are in a prison anyway. They don't do things that cross the line of criminal activity, but their lives are just as much a mess as those who do.

For the purpose of self-examination, I offer here a list of things that can be considered fruits of the problem. If you honestly have ever been guilty of even just one in this list, the fundamental question is: How does this feeling manifest itself in your life?

Have you ever fallen short of God's best through self-importance, disobedience, willfulness, self-righteousness, or seeking approval and praise? Have you ever been felled by pride, narcissism, conceit, envy, love of praise, honors, or putting on airs? You think no one notices because you're successful, glib, and street smart. But others see through you like glass. They may give you a pass, but you're not fooling anyone. Some people are guilty of abuse or insults, and others have a euphoric recall of previous sins. Some exhibit arrogant behavior, insolence, lack of respect, judgment, malicious gossip, anger, grudges, hatred, slander, lies, slyness, deception, hypocrisy, prejudices, or stubbornness to list a few. Surely everyone has been guilty at one time or another of one of these behaviors. It's called being human. Many times people require professional help and medication. For me many of these "problem fruits" left me feeling that no one in the world could truly understand me or would ever know what I was all about. That is surely a recipe for loneliness and depression.

As the Lord is my witness, when I asked Jesus into my life, the last thing I was thinking about was salvation. I wasn't looking to cop a plea in the hope God would have mercy on me and have me avoid prison. I needed immediate help, help in so many ways that I couldn't begin to list them. Some I was aware of, most I wasn't. Dying would have been easy. I needed help in being able to live my life here on earth. I still do. Aside from Harvey, I needed to have a personal relationship with a God so personal that he knit me together in my mother's womb. Since he made me, I had full confidence he could repair me. Because he loves me so unconditionally, I have always been confident he *would* repair me. I've continually failed, but I repent, attempt to make things right, and move forward.

After coming to Christ, I found it an absolute necessity to get alone and talk to him in prayer and pour out my heart. I came to understand that Jesus himself had the same problem when among us. No one really knew what he was about. Even the ones living and traveling with him on a daily basis could not come to grips with the entire truth of his personhood. He must have felt he was walking the halls of an insane asylum, where no one was able to truly relate to or understand him. The human part of Jesus made him depart from everyone to be alone with God the Father as only he could still Jesus's restless heart.

In the middle of my times of crisis or the time I spent in prison, I didn't need to be a scriptural scholar to understand I needed help and be alone with God. However, I've been out of prison since 1980, and sometimes when things appear to be going well, I forget that I'm shouldering an unnecessary burden through worry and concern, when God never intended me to live that way. It's the height of ego for me to even entertain the thought that my good efforts or intentions ever control anything. It was for these reasons I invited Christ in to my life in the first place. I truly believe that all good and perfect gifts come from him. However, out of prison with worldly responsibilities demanding so much time and effort, I find it's so easy to forget our need of him.

But when I meet people like Larry, I remember all over again.

# Chapter 33

# LESSONS FROM LARRY

I met Larry in a high-security California prison. Apparently, he was a computer savant who thought he could rob an employer with impunity.

What a horrible place. Once past the high outside walls, guard towers, razor wire, and armed men shouldering rifles, Harvey and I entered a large waiting room crowded with people going through the painstaking entry process to visit a loved one. They all appeared to be low-income families, and their faces evidenced the no-hope look I've seen so often when visiting prisons. My heart and prayers went out to each of them.

Once inside, we were herded to a large recreation room with picnic-style benches and vending machines on all four walls. Guards were positioned everywhere. Larry's mom had told him what I would be wearing so he would be able to know I was the person visiting. Larry was a good-looking man, probably twenty-six years old. I knew the vending machines held a treasure trove of tasty treats not otherwise available on the inside. I spent several dollars on chips, candy, and coffee, and we sat down to visit. Eventually Larry got down to what was on his mind. He told of all the injustices in his life and of unforgiveness and rage toward his parents. I listened for half an hour to his litany of complaints.

"Larry, you're twenty-six. Suppose I told you that I knew for certain the next twenty-six years of your life would be no better than the first twenty-six. You're an intelligent guy. If you knew you'd have another twenty-six years of living in a zoo like this, wouldn't the most rational decision you'd make be how and when to kill yourself? Doesn't it seem logical to end the torment?" My style may be somewhat abhorrent to proponents of friendship evangelism. This is only to say there are different methods for different folks. Like a mule, some need a hit over the head with a two-by-four just to get their attention. Since coming to Christ, I have always had a heart for the lost and believe God's word that "now is the day of salvation" (2 Corinthians 6:2), and today is the day to be saved. On that, Joe the Butcher and I agree and leave friendship evangelism to others.

Larry asked Jesus into his heart. For the rest of the time he remained in prison, he and his mother had a true reconciliation of spirits. Once home he attended Bible studies and prayer groups and was a model son and citizen. But the end of the story is that Larry fell to temptations of the flesh and seems to have disappeared from the face of the earth. My guess is that he's incarcerated somewhere, with his dear Christian mother continuing to miss him on the outside and love him as only a mother can.

Some might feel that a true conversion to Christ means we are incapable of returning to a sinful way of life. That is not true. Some might say that he was never saved in the first place. That's only for the Lord to know. What I do know is that within God's sovereignty, every moment of every day we are called to make decisions based on the free will the Lord has allowed us. The Evil One is real and roams around seeking someone to devour. My prayer continues to be for those who have fallen away and have not repented. Whether in or out of prison, I know of no one more miserable than a person out of the fellowship of God, especially one of his.

# Chapter 34

# TWO BIG DECISIONS

The two most important decisions a person will ever make—much greater than what house to purchase, where to send children to school, what career to pursue, or what car to drive—is with whom to spend eternity and with whom to spend the rest of one's earthly life. I have made the correct decision on both counts.

When I first met Harvey, it was love at first sight. I recall a time before our marrying when we went to Grossinger's Hotel in the Catskill Mountains of New York State, where she had a modeling assignment. Claude and Linda joined us for the weekend, and we were seated for dinner in a cavernous room. Sometime during the meal, I excused myself to go to the men's room. On my return, I crossed the huge expanse of floor to get back to our booth, against a far wall. I looked across the room and saw Harvey. She was absolutely beautiful, perhaps the most stunning female I had ever viewed. I was so proud to be with her and to be the one people would see crossing the room to sit next to her. When I returned we kissed, and I thought my heart would explode from sheer joy. At the time, Harvey was twenty-two and I was twenty-eight.

On our forty-seventh anniversary, I wrote one attribute for each year of our marriage that I loved about her when we were dating and still do today. One was: "My heart is gladdened when I see you enter a room." And it's true to this day! But as extensive as my list is, how could I have imagined the enormity of her love, loyalty, faithfulness, steely resolve, work ethic, and being a true savant when it comes to knowing what vitamin pills to dispense? How could I possibly know the problem solver she turned out to be or the extent of her godly influence on so many? There's a good bit of silver in her hair these days, and she wears glasses all the time. Her beauty has matured inside and out. Though she doesn't suffer fools gladly, she remains my best friend and the kindest person I have ever known.

Harvey writes, "After forty-seven years, I know Stephen Lawson better than anyone else on the face of the earth. Although everything he shares in this book is true, I testify to the fact he isn't any more perfect than I am. We both have our own idiosyncrasies, but we like each other's quirks, and it works for us. I think that he sometimes mumbles although he says my hearing is bad; he's prone to being impatient; and he interrupts too much because he's convinced he knows what you're about to say. There are times he hovers and can be like a Boy Scout who wants to help a lady cross the street even when she doesn't want to go. Further, he has a love-hate relationship with technology and can cause a computer to freeze up just by looking at it.

"That aside, from the first day we met, Stephen and I have had a wonderful relationship and life together even though there were those eighteen-months he spent in Florida. We never had a problem communicating and sharing our feelings, and I have always loved and liked him. Stephen has a fabulous sense of humor, and our life is filled with laughter no matter the circumstances. This isn't to say every day is a box of chocolates, because poor decisions still cause poor results. Sometimes it's no more than just being caught in the crossfire of life in a fallen world. I testify to the fact he is a totally changed person because of Christ and the indwelling Holy Spirit. However great our relationship was before, it can't compare to what we have now. The hallmark of our lives is contentment in all circumstances and being at peace. Forgiveness lives at the Lawson household."

The best marriages are ones where the husband and wife tell each other on a daily basis how much they love each other. They acknowledge and own their faults, and they apologize and ask forgiveness when necessary. Additionally, most couples recall something their spouse did in an especially thoughtful way that said they were loved.

It's no less true in your relationship with God and the way he loves you.

Early on in our Christian life, I was in the pits when Harvey and I attended a healing service at the Cathedral of St. Philip conducted by Fr. Zampino, a well-known

Episcopal priest with an international healing ministry. I was taken with his humility and the fact he was under the authority of his bishop who always traveled with him. At one point in the service, Fr. Zampino felt led to come into the congregation and lay hands on certain people and pray specifically for their needs based on individual words of knowledge for each. Everyone was kneeling in prayer. Harvey and I were in the back third of the church pews on the right side. Fr. Zampino laid hands on someone in the first row and then seemed to crawl over people to lay hands on someone in the fourth row. This zigzag continued for over twenty minutes until he was about ten rows in front of us. I was feeling especially sorry for myself and prayed several times "Lord, please don't forget me." In a flash Fr. Zampino bypassed those rows in front of me and came midway down the row in which we were seated. This man who had never seen me before laid hands on me and prayed fervently for those very things I was experiencing in my life. The fog of failure vanished along with any fear of the future. Fr. Zampino exhorted me to believe God for every opinion he had of me and not to despair. As much as I appreciated the prayer, I also appreciated how the Lord heard the longing of my heart and rushed in to say how much he loved me. I know of nothing better than the love of a spouse wrapped in the love of God.

*Chapter 35*

# REPENTANCE AND FORGIVENESS

S ome have no doubt when it comes to the Lord's readiness to physically heal. Others have difficulty trusting God for finances or for healing wounded emotions. Others know exactly their root problems but keep taking back what God already dealt with at the cross. The old hurts may not have completely vanished because it may be a process. Some people may persistently disregard their ability through Christ to heal spiritually and instead continue in their old habits and painful ways. The human condition is complicated, and all of us Christians continue to be a work in progress.

In one way or the other, we've all gone through the school of hard knocks. Someone says a word or shows an expression that reminds us of a hurtful time from our past. One feels injured all over again, and the adolescent, now grown old, rises to defend itself. That attitude can make others want to flee. But as Christians we don't have to live that way anymore. For example, I started to believe God was right about me and that Mother was wrong. How understandable it all seems now! How could I have been so influenced by someone so critical and unkind, someone who never exhibited any peace in her own life? Basically, she was a victim of a victim, and I allowed myself to be one as well. How does one come to grips with something like that? In the first chapter of *Daddy* I wrote how I made peace with my Dad, who had died many years earlier. Looking at his picture, I apologized for the thoughts I had held against him. I experienced release and closure. The matter was settled by my understanding that Mother and Dad did the best they were able. *Period. Case closed.*

Harvey has excellent insights on this: "Forgiveness is a process for the Christian, and it takes not only your willingness to forgive, but perhaps more importantly, it requires the power of the Holy Spirit to initiate your need to forgive and give you the ability to complete the process. Completing the journey removes the sting and pain and enables you to joyfully go forward. The truth is, none of us is good enough or perfected enough in our own strength to be able to say, "I forgive you" and make it permanent, even when we really want to forgive. When old hurts and issues bubble back up into our consciousness, at that moment, we have to take authority over the thought or feeling by asking the help of the Holy Spirit. I would say, "Lord, I forgave him or her of all things past, and I truly do not want to dwell on those issues again. Please give me the ability to release him or her to your safe keeping." Then I'd begin to pray for the person who was causing me angst, asking the Lord to bless, heal, restore, and fill any void in their life. Does it happen all at once the first time we pray to forgive someone? I would say, usually, no. I can only speak from my personal experience and say it is a process. If at first you don't succeed, and you probably won't, then redouble your efforts. You are asking God for a change of heart—your heart. The person you are forgiving may not change, but you are asking God to restore peace in your own heart. As long as you retain anger, bitterness, or resentment in your heart, there will be no peace with God.

"Five years before Stephen went to prison, he went to the SEC and laid out his problems regarding the 6-J exemptions for the private-placement offerings and signed a statement outlining the issues as he saw them. His meeting and his statement were quietly leaked to the newspaper. The next day when the story hit the front page above the fold, Stephen was basically out of business. The reality that his business life was over didn't hit immediately, and it was a slow death. Timing is everything, they say, and it was just two months short of the statute of limitations running out on Stephen's issue with the SEC when they indicted him. There were basically five years where we tried to piece things together financially and restore our lives because we had lost our business, investments, reputation, social life, and friends. We had made a promise to be kind to each other in spite of the circumstances. I found a good job that fit my skills: director of a fine arts center in Atlanta. I became compulsive in my work, and when I wasn't there, I thought about it every hour of every day. I unknowingly used it as a camouflage to hide my pain. I did not comprehend how deep the hurts were from the loneliness and emptiness I experienced from the lack of friends. We had run in the fast lane, and it was obvious to us now that we had fair-weather friends. We truly liked them, and they were fun, but our situation personified 'out of sight, out of mind.'

"Our story of crying out to God is told in the earlier portion of the book, but I'll say here that it was nothing short of a first-class miracle. God met us at the exact point where we could go no further in our own strength. We were done. As you remember Stephen flew to Lexington, Kentucky, to see an investor, but really his intention was suicide. I told him I was just a spent piece of elastic and had no more give. I could not spring back. What I did not share in the original book was how I journeyed to genuine forgiveness and from forgiveness to the restoration of our relationship.

"Stephen and I both devoured the Word of God. Neither he nor I could put our Bibles down. The truth and wisdom that poured forth from those pages were phenomenal. It seemed as if every chapter I read, I ran into the word *forgive* or *forgiveness*, starting in Genesis going through the Old Testament to the New Testament. Verses like this especially stood out: '"I ask you to forgive your brothers the sins and the wrongs they committed in treating you so badly." Now please forgive the sins of the servants of the God of your father.' When their message came to him, Joseph wept" [Genesis 50:17].

"I encountered verse after verse relating to or mentioning forgiveness. Then I read, '"If you forgive others when they sin against you, your heavenly Father will also forgive you. But if you do not forgive others their sins, your Father will not forgive you"'" [Matthew 6:14–15].

"And, then there was this verse in Colossians 3:12–14, 'Therefore, as God's chosen people, holy and dearly loved, clothe yourselves with compassion, kindness, humility, gentleness and patience. Bear with each other and forgive one another if any of you has a grievance against someone. Forgive as the Lord forgave you. And over all these virtues put on love, which binds them all together in perfect unity.' The Lord knew my deep need to truly forgive, and he made sure that I didn't miss one Scripture verse that would lead me to the conclusion that these Scriptures were meant for me!

"I forgave Stephen long before he left for prison. I clearly recognized my own sinful condition and knew beyond a doubt that the Lord had forgiven me and wiped the slate clean through the shed blood of Jesus Christ. We could not continue in our marriage nor face the consequences ahead without genuine, unconditional forgiveness. I had to surrender my right to be right; my right to be angry; my right to make unloving or unkind remarks, and most especially my right to take back those things I said I had forgiven! Once forgiven, the issue must be released to God knowing that the Holy Spirit will empower you to keep your word. Never make a vow that you don't plan to keep as it is better not to make the vow at all than to make it and take it back. The same applies to forgiveness.

"In all honestly, I had a few starts and stops, but each time something welled up in me—anger, resentment, or bitterness—I knew I had to go to the Lord immediately to confess that I was taking back those things I had forgiven. I asked for the indwelling power of the Holy Spirit to give me the grace to forgive Stephen as the Lord had forgiven me. Of course that is the key to this whole issue: God has forgiven each of us for so much, so how can we not forgive others, particularly when they have repented before you and God and truly desire your forgiveness. The most difficult times to forgive are when the other person is unrepentant and doesn't care about the pain they've inflicted. Or when a loved one is murdered or killed on the battlefield or by a drunk driver.

"Stephen and I had always been best friends. I didn't just love him; I liked him, and there was no one's company I preferred over his. And during all our difficult times before becoming Christians, I didn't complain or demean my husband in public, privately to family members, or in a conversation with a girlfriend. I have never understood women who complain about their husbands to others. Mumbling and complaining publicly about the person you have married only leads to your spouse having bitter and deceitful thoughts, which will probably be acted upon later. I strongly suggest that when one needs to vent or complain, if the situation merits it go to your pastor or a family counselor. Keep family and friends out of the situation for obvious reasons. If a person solves the difficulty and the marriage is back in a good place, family or friends will surely remember all the negative things said about the spouse."

Make no mistake; repentance does not mean restoration. Restoration of a relationship must happen over a period of time. It's important to recognize where those areas of trust are so important to your spouse and do everything you can to advance the process. I believe Harvey will attest that I did everything within my ability to give her confidence in my actions.

Harvey recalls: "I never really imagined Stephen would ever gamble again, but once he came home, he totally surrendered the checkbook to me so that I could never hold doubt about any flow of money. When he was paid a salary, he endorsed his paychecks, and I deposited them into my account. Once direct deposit came along, it was even easier. As a matter of fact, he hasn't been a signatory on a bank account since he returned from prison. Ever since that time, I have paid all the bills and been the family manager of funds for our personal account and the corporate accounts. Stephen has just one credit card, and the billing comes to my attention each month. From the beginning, I never considered there to be a gap between Stephen's repentance and restoration of my trust. However, with twenty-twenty hindsight, I believe it was due to my complete trust of the Lord having done a mighty work in his life. After all, I know what he has done in mine."

Similarly, a persistent connection remains between the consequence of former sin and our present situation— even though we have been forgiven by God, by those we have wronged, and even by ourselves. Consider the case of Philip, a fall-down drunk unable or unwilling to stay sober. One day he had an epiphany, and his life turned upside down. It was truly a miracle. Of that, no one would doubt. He lived the rest of his life in peace and repentance. However, all that didn't stop his dying from cirrhosis of the liver as a consequence of former sin. Admittedly, this is a classic example, but any ex-felon can expect this reality in other forms. Some may never trust you again because of their preconceived notions that you'll always be the same person, unable to change. Christians aren't absolved from this type thinking. This is where believing God comes in, believing what he thinks about you and his unyielding love for you as opposed to other negative perceptions.

# Chapter 36

# NOT A SPECTATOR SPORT

B eing a Christian is not a spectator sport. You have to get in the game and get your jersey dirty. The future is for those who plan for the road ahead while cleaning up the debris from the road behind. This is a time-consuming process and not to be entered into by wimps because 100 percent of the time the past includes either asking for forgiveness or extending forgiveness. If you have accepted forgiveness, it is incumbent upon you to accept it and hold tight. Your forgiveness isn't negotiable to God. He won't take back what he's forgiven. And if you again take on the burden of being unforgiven, you stray out of the will of God. You have placed your emotions in a higher position than you allowed the Lord to occupy. How egotistical can a person be?

On the other hand, your seeking forgiveness by others is no less important. Make no mistake, although the person you apologize to may appreciate the gesture, your spiritual need to apologize is always greater than another's need to receive it. That's the key here. Please recall that the first people I apologized to were my former attorneys—the very ones who didn't file my partnership papers with the SEC in a timely way. It started a legal process that ended up sending me to prison. I am not saying I wasn't guilty, because clearly I was. However, an argument can be made that if attention wasn't drawn to my activities through their misfeasance, I might have swum past the net. My feeling was they were responsible for 95 percent of the legal action that began. The problem is that God doesn't grade on the curve. The 5 percent I admitted to was 100 percent of the problem the Lord wanted me to deal with. I wrote and apologized for my character assassination by the unkind things I said about them to others. I apologized to them for the hatred I felt and my desire to have awful things happen to them. Basically I apologized for what in good conscience I knew I was guilty of. How they accepted it, I do not know. I do know that no amount of money in the world could purchase the new feeling of peace and joy I experienced. Our relationship with God is easy to understand once we have become Christians. He establishes a pattern for us to follow. We sin, we genuinely repent, and God forgive us. Now when others sin against us we are to forgive them—as God forgives us. Don't forgive others—he doesn't forgive you. These issues of forgiveness have nothing at all to do with your salvation. It is an issue of fellowship. Situations where we are tardy in forgiving others only means our fellowship with the Lord is disturbed. During those times we tend to feel uneasy and anxious. Forgiving others equates to peace within the soul.

Harvey shares, "When Stephen came home from prison, Blake was close to seven years old. We both realized that he had to apologize to his son for being in prison and the shame it must have caused him with his schoolmates. Stephen got together with Blake and asked his forgiveness, and Blake said he forgave him. One would think, mission accomplished. But then Blake said he was so glad Daddy was home because he felt very bad last year when it was Father and Son Day at school, and he felt so alone. He went on, not at all in an unkind way, to tell of other things that had happened; for example, what a particular classmate had said. Blake had a long list and Stephen gave me a look that expressed Blake's laundry list would never end. When it did, Stephen spoke to each of the matters Blake had brought up and asked forgiveness for each, item by item rather than just saying he was sorry in a general sort of way. He wanted Blake to realize he had been heard and that each instance had received an apology. It's vitally important to apologize with specificity and say you are sorry for the broken trust and hurt they felt, item by item. He did the same with me."

I had several hundred past investors. I wrote each of them and shared how I was sorry I turned out to be unworthy of their trust, and sorry that they lost their investments. That accomplished, I knew I had done everything within my power to be at peace with all people. I prayed for each person and released each one to God to bless, and I released any negative opinions those persons held of me to God. If God loves me, who can be against me? It's not an arrogant perspective; it's a Biblical perspective.

Let's reverse the process. Has someone ever offended you for reasons either real or imagined? You must go to them. Explain that your mutual relationship is so important to you that you don't want anything to impair it, and on that basis bring the issue to their attention. Allow them an opportunity to bring closure.

Remember the most important point: Your forgiveness does not excuse the person's action. You never have to do that. You choose, by an act of your will, to forgive the person in spite of his or her actions. Once this is done, the one extending forgiveness has no right to ever bring it up again or respond in a way that suggests forgiveness never happened. Extending forgiveness forfeits that behavior as an option.

Several years ago, Harvey and I were invited to a large event for the Atlanta Opera held at a patron's lovely estate. It was on an evening during the middle of May. The weather was clear, with a comfortable 70 degrees and low humidity. The silent auction was on our host's extremely large back patio, now heavily populated with people examining donated items awaiting their bids. The expansive lawn held tables able to seat four as they sipped wine and enjoyed the evening. Further down there was a bridge that led to an island within their backyard. On the island a dance floor had been assembled, and an orchestra played.

A friend of Blake's approached to say hello and introduced me to his girlfriend. Her dad had been a member of the Friday morning prayer group but no longer attended because he was living in a care facility. I inquired how he was doing, and we chatted about him for a few moments prior to their leaving to be with others. Fifteen minutes later, Blake's friend returned to tell me that I had terribly offended his date over something I had said. It was easy to discern he was upset. "Oh, I feel terrible," I said. "Where is she now?" He showed me the table she was sitting at all alone and I immediately went over and sat down next to her.

"Janet, Bill told me I said something to offend you when we were taking about your dad. I can't tell you how badly I feel because your dad means a great deal to me."

"That's okay."

"No, it really isn't. I hurt your feelings, and I can't begin to tell you how badly I feel. Please accept my apology in the knowledge I've always loved your dad."

"Sure. Okay. Thanks," she said.

"Janet, I'm not leaving this table until you smile and tell me I'm forgiven. The only way to get rid of me is to say you and I are okay and for us to stand up and share a hug." After my hug, Bill seemingly appeared from nowhere. I bid my goodbye, and returned to Harvey.

How grateful I was that Bill felt confident enough in me to approach so I might make something right. Was Janet overly sensitive or having a very bad day and taken something completely out of context and totally wrong? I don't know, and it doesn't matter. I never intended any of my remarks about her dad to be offensive. Even if what I said was true, it didn't take away from the fact her feelings had been hurt. Who is that someone in your life?

So I end this chapter the same way I started it. Being a Christian isn't a spectator sport, and it isn't intended for wimps. ". . . and let us run with endurance the race that is set before us fixing our eyes on Jesus, the author and perfecter of faith . . ." (Hebrews 12:1-2)

And sometimes being a Christian takes unexpected turns. Our coming turn was huge.

# Chapter 37

# A NEW ANCIENT SPIRITUAL HOME

During Blake's freshman year at Westmont College in Santa Barbara, California, Harvey and I made one of our trips to the West Coast to get our "kid fix." A mother is particularly happy when she can put eyes on her kid, college-age or not. And thanks to our being in the travel business, we could fly out to California more frequently than we could have otherwise. Harvey had been reading the *Christian Activist: A Journal of Orthodox Opinion*, a quarterly newspaper published by Franky Shaeffer, son of Francis Shaeffer, noted Protestant theologian who founded L'Abri in Switzerland.

Franky Shaeffer had converted to the Eastern Orthodox Church, and his articles intrigued Harvey. She called the *Activist* and asked if there was an Orthodox church in Santa Barbara because we might like to visit one on our trip to see Blake. They suggested St. Athanasius Antiochian Orthodox Church in Isla Vista by the University of California Santa Barbara (UCSB), about ten miles from Westmont College.

Harvey remembers: "We arrived in Santa Barbara on a Thursday afternoon looking forward to a long, wonderful visit with Blake, our only child. Santa Barbara is like la-la land and often described as California's answer to the French Riviera. It was one of those picturesque weekends with cloudless skies and a cool breeze. While we were lunching in an outdoor café with a profusion of bougainvillea cascading over flower boxes and a heady perfume from all the blooming flowers, I brought up going to this unknown Orthodox church on Sunday. Stephen and Blake reminded me that we had reservations at a fabulous restaurant on Saturday night and would be getting back late, so we should probably just sleep in on Sunday. We never miss church—either Blake or us—but it seemed to them a reasonable idea that we could miss this Sunday. Of course we wanted to enjoy a leisurely Sunday brunch at another fabulous Santa Barbara restaurant and then head on down to Los Angeles to catch our flight home early Monday morning. So I let it go. However, I brought up the subject again on Saturday afternoon. I asked them just to pamper me and agree to go to this church on Sunday morning. They agreed. And the rest is history!

"St. Athanasius is a unpretentious freestanding building and doesn't really look like the typical church. We entered not knowing what to expect and heard a cappella chanting coming from a side area. There were icons everywhere, and the smell of incense permeated the space. They used metal folding chairs like so many storefront nondenominational churches, but this was truly different. There was an altar, a liturgy that sounded ancient, priests in full-length brocade robes, and of course, the chanting going back and forth antiphonally between the priests and the chanters. The liturgy was entirely of Scripture so that the Word of God simply poured over you throughout the service; it incorporated Old and New Testament verses, and the poetic structure of the liturgy was extraordinary. It engaged us immediately as it activated all of our senses and kept us attentive. The entire service pointed us to receive the body and blood of Christ represented by the sacraments, to receive Christ, to invite him into our life, and to receive his life-giving gifts. I had taken Communion in the Episcopal Church since I was confirmed as a twelve-year old, but I had never experienced anything quite like this in any church. All I could say was wow. I was overwhelmed by the dignity and reverence the service generated. It was so different from what we knew and yet so appealing.

"Blake turned to me in the service and said, 'I don't know what you and Dad are going to do, but I've just found my church home!' Stephen and I were in awe, and obviously so was Blake.

"We realized during the service we could not participate in the sacraments, but the priest invited all non-Orthodox to come forward to receive a blessing. After the service ended a lovely church member greeted us in the narthex. We introduced ourselves and said we were visiting from Atlanta. She introduced herself as Marilyn Gillquist and said there was an Atlanta connection to this church and she wanted us to meet Deacon Howard Shannon and his wife, Gail. Gail and I struck up a conversation and covered the bases of where we went to school in Atlanta and where our families lived. I knew exactly where her parents lived and remembered attending a party there while in high school.

She and her sister, Yetty, are a bit younger than I am, but they had a good-looking brother who held the party, and I was there!

"Marilyn invited us to her home for lunch, where we discovered that she was *Presbytera* Marilyn, a title of honor given to a woman married to a priest. Fr. Peter Gillquist, author of *Becoming Orthodox: A Journey to the Ancient Faith* is *Presbytera* Marilyn's husband. But the story gets better: Before Peter Gillquist became an Orthodox priest, he was an acquisitions editor at Thomas Nelson Books. Our friend Victor Oliver, who directed the Oliver-Nelson book division at Thomas Nelson, arranged for us to meet Peter Gillquist to discuss Stephen's manuscript. He ended up spending the night at our home so that we could further discuss our story of coming to Christ and Stephen's journey in prison."

Blake found his church home, but we returned to Atlanta on a search mission. We were divided in our thinking because we were members of a believing, right-thinking Episcopal Church. Fr. Frank Balser was a wonderful, loving priest at St. Jude's, and we were involved with Episcopal Renewal Ministries (ERM). Fr. Charlie Fulton headed up the ministry of ERM, and his wife, Judy, was one of my all-time favorite people and a dear, close friend. Nevertheless, we began visiting Orthodox churches in Atlanta. For anyone who is not Greek, not Middle Eastern, or not Russian, it could be problematic as to where to begin. When ethnic populations arrived in America, if they were churchgoers in their native country, they found a church where their language was spoken and their culture honored. Stephen's parents were Jewish, his father originally from England and his mom from Kentucky. My family tree showed generations living in the United States, and I did not relate to any ethic group. Our best choice, it seemed, was to find a service conducted in English.

We visited churches from one end of Atlanta to another. English may have been spoken at the coffee hour, but services were in the original language of the founding members. One of our dear Greek friends said to us, "Why do you want to attend that church; you aren't Greek!" We laughed together about it because our friend did not mean to be off-putting, just realistic, and thankfully his statement did not deter us from our journey. At last we found a church where the service was almost entirely in English, and the priest was Canadian. We continued to visit weekly and then called to inquire about joining the church as we assumed we would just get a letter of transfer from the Episcopal Church to the Antiochian Orthodox Church.

We found, however, that we needed to attend weekly catechism classes while attending services before we could go through the chrismation service to become members. The church was willing to accept our baptism, but they made the assumption that we knew nothing or next to nothing about church history and tradition, and they were correct! In the beginning we felt as if they discounted our years of Bible study and our love for the Word, but we plowed ahead even though it seemed difficult at the time. Finally, after more than a year of classes, we still had not been allowed to receive the sacraments, and we thought we were no closer to becoming Orthodox—or at least it seemed that way.

Stephen went to the priest and in his direct, cut-to-the-chase style said, "Enough is enough. We want to be chrismated and brought into the church, and we want a certain date!" Stephen reminded our priest that as a Jewish believer, he had given up a lot to become a Christian and asked our priest not to deny or delay this any longer. Stephen reminded him that "hope deferred makes the heart sick" (Proverbs 13:12). In looking back on that time, Stephen and I believe the priest made a right decision because this is a major change. Our priest just wanted to assure himself of our commitment and to make sure this decision would not be taken lightly. It is not just a simple change of attendance from your old church to a new church several miles away or a change of denomination like going from the Presbyterian to Methodist. Christians today are always moving around from denomination to denomination and even beyond to nondenominational congregations or to being a part of a group that is starting a new church. Our priest wanted assurance that we were totally serious in our pledge and intent. And the passage of time can be the best judge of a person's word.

Stephen and I knew we wanted to be a part of this ancient faith, which had no broken line for almost two thousand years. We felt strongly that this is where we belonged. We were willing to let go of our comfortable surroundings in our local church and the familiar teachings in order to learn more and draw closer to God from the original church perspective. We had read extensively and attended classes faithfully, and we were ready. About a month after Stephen's conversation with our priest, our chrismation was scheduled around the period known as the Dormition, which is a period in the church year around August 15 honoring the passing away of the Virgin Mary.

It was a Saturday in August 1996 like any Saturday, except that it was the Saturday before the feast of the Dormition of the Theotokos (the falling asleep of Mary, the mother and God-bearer of Christ), which our priest felt was an appropriate time for our chrismation service. We had three church sponsors, which is something similar to godparents. As the service began, the priest met us in the narthex and escorted us into the church while he chanted a beautiful prayer, and the service began.

No service in the Orthodox Church is short. I think those who created the services almost two centuries ago took their cue from the Old Testament in that God repeats statements and thoughts multiple times with the intent that the reader or hearer will therefore get it. In the chrismation service we make an oath to God and to his church, both now and always, and one should not enter into this lightly.

If you would like to see the Chrismation service format, I have included it as an appendix.

# Chapter 38

# ADJUSTING TO OUR NEW PATH

In Protestant church life, changing churches or denominations is always a gut-wrenching decision as you are leaving old friends behind as well as the familiar liturgy and
style of your church. It was obvious in the Orthodox Church
you don't do that. In our past we saw church members
who disagreed with the pastor, got mad at church leaders,
or just felt that this church was no longer a good fit, and
they moved on; but it would not be so now. We had made
a major decision in our spiritual lives and had taken an
vow in the chrismation service, and we clearly recognized
that God takes vows very seriously. We believed then as
we believe today that we made a wonderful choice. We
wanted the historical tie to the early church. Most of us
in the Protestant faith can only trace church history back to
Luther and the breakaway from the Roman Catholic
Church, if that. Of course, Luther had no way of knowing
the future or realizing that his act of disagreement with the
Roman Catholic Church would bring about the unintended
consequences of between twenty-five thousand to fifty

thousand denominations and sects forming since his decision on October 31, 1517.

We have been Orthodox since 1996, and we did make a change from the Antiochian Orthodox Church to the Greek Orthodox Church due only to our moving. Our priest at the time made the suggestion that we move to Holy Transfiguration Greek Orthodox Church, closer to our new home. The liturgical service is the same whether you attend a Greek, Antiochian, Russian, or any canonical Orthodox church. All use the liturgy of St. John Chrysostom, which was compiled and formalized in the years AD 398–404.

Harvey and I agree that our years in the Protestant Church were wonderful, with strong friendships and incredibly wonderful teaching. Atlanta is blessed with great churches, pastors, and Bible teachers. We will always feel grateful for our pastors, past and present, for the Monday night prayer and praise group at the Cathedral, as well as for the conferences and weekend retreats. Harvey and I are also grateful for the teaching and pastoring we received beyond our own wonderful church. We were blessed by the Rev. Charles Stanley, In Touch Ministries, Kay Arthur Ministries, the Rev. Gray Temple, the Rev. Charlie Fulton, the Rev. Frank Balser, and Ken Boa of Reflections Ministries, to name a few.

But there was something missing, and it was not until reading about the ancient church through the *Christian Activist* and then attending the Orthodox service in Santa Barbara that we realized we were missing the link to the ancient church. "Church," we discovered, was more than great sermons, praise with exuberant music, and singing. It is sacramental, liturgical, traditional, conservative, and historical. It is worship that instills awe, majesty, and mystery. Just as the Scriptures are totally connected from Genesis to Revelation, there is also an unbroken connection from the original church to today. Maybe for us it was middle age wishing for dignity and decorum, but then how do I explain Blake as a freshman in college? It hit all three of us the same way on that Sunday in Isla Vista. The Orthodox Church is the original church. The liturgy has not changed in almost two thousand years. We don't have to try and create it; it's here, healthy and strong. Truly, our journey as evangelical Christians prepared our hearts and minds for our encounter with the Orthodox Church.

Honestly, I couldn't put it into words and explain it that day. Intuitively it was just right, and the three of us knew it. We loved the Lord, and we knew we were loved by him. His Word planted deeply into our hearts, we were hungry for the fullness of the Orthodox Church and its connection to the original church handed down from apostle to bishop to priest for nearly two thousand years.

For Blake the experience was much easier, and he fit right into the convert-oriented congregation at Santa Barbara. It was made up of Protestants who were part of a group of churches from San Diego to San Francisco that had been accepted into the Antiochian Orthodox Church as a group. The service was in English, and most of the congregation had previously been evangelicals. Originally the priests from these various West Coast churches had come out of leadership positions within Campus Crusade for Christ, and Gillquist's *Becoming Orthodox* is the wonderful story of how twenty-five hundred people were accepted into the Orthodox Church. It was not an easy journey for them! These men were more than overcomers and totally trusted God through the entire up-and-down, lengthy process.

Today there are many, many converts in the Orthodox Church, but when we visited churches many years ago, converts were more the exception than the rule. The Antiochian Churches then were primarily made up of Lebanese and Syrian families, and hospitality was a given from people who come from that part of the world. The congregation was very friendly and welcoming. However, once we started going frequently to a particular church, one of the regular church ladies took Harvey aside and asked, "What are your roots?" Honestly, Harvey didn't understand what she was asking her at first, and the lady said it again, "What are your roots?"

Harvey flippantly responded, "I was born blonde, but I do help it along now and then.

The church member gave her a look that would bend steel.

"Forgive me," Harvey said, "what exactly do you mean?"

"Your family derivation—where do your relatives come from?"

"Well," I said, "my mother's family has been here since before the American Revolution, but my maiden name is Reinhard, which is of German derivation, so does that answer your question?" We never discussed my roots again.

Nothing worthwhile ever comes easily. But we persevered as we believed it was what the Lord would have us do. We have never looked back. We belong to a wonderful congregation, Holy Transfiguration Greek Orthodox Church, with a priest we love who is originally from Cyprus; his wife, Catherine, a Floridian is also a convert as well as his precious mother-in-law, Nancy. We love them and their grown children, Strati and Olympia. We are grateful for their friendship and wisdom.

Harvey remains a part of a wonderful Bible study group known as The Grapenuts—Protestants from various denominations, and women of great integrity and biblical wisdom. Their only desire is to know Jesus better and better.

Frederica Mathewes-Green, a convert to Orthodoxy and wife of an Orthodox priest, has written extensively on the subject of Orthodoxy and sums up our feelings well from her book, *Welcome to the Orthodox Church, An Introduction to Eastern Christianity.* "Ever since I became a Christian, forty years ago, I have been longing to know the Lord better. That's all I want: to get closer to him, to be always in his presence, to see everywhere his work and know his will. I feel a strong connection with Christians everywhere who have this longing, no matter what church they attend. Drawing nearer to Jesus is the most important thing."

Harvey echoes Green's thoughts when she writes, "The Grapenuts group is so much more than an inductive Bible study. We pray for each other, and I have been truly blessed by their prayers, as well as their cooking, which sustained Blake and me through many difficult days."

*Chapter 39*

# BLAKE'S TAKE: OUR JOURNEY TO ORTHODOXY

*Because our move to the Orthodox Church was so significant, I've included a chapter from Blake's perspective.*

The word *orthodox* can be most simply defined as correct or right thinking. It was being non-orthodox in his thinking and actions that landed Dad in the slammer. By the grace of God, Dad came to right thinking and actions by eliminating the use of situational ethics. How he arrived at this point was by reading the Holy Scriptures, both Old and New Testaments, and his commitment to follow the teachings of Jesus Christ, the apostles, and the saints.

We began our Christian life in the Episcopal Church and were fortunate to have wonderful pastors and teachers. What left our family scratching our heads from time to time was why one particular church seemed to be theologically sound but the Episcopal church a mile down the road was not. Why were Christian denominations at odds with each other over doctrine, dogma, spiritual practice, tradition, and the like? We also attended a very well-known and respected Baptist church in Atlanta for several years that had fantastic spiritual and life application teachings but lacked historical church tradition. Then there are the churches that Dad called the "Church of What's Happening Now, Baby," and just like fads, they come and go. Or we heard of pastors at one church starting to disagree and bicker, and before one knew it, the congregation took sides and the church split with one of the pastors taking a large chunk of the congregation to start a new church. There is nothing worse than when the body of Christ, the church, is at odds with itself.

As of 2012 there were twenty-five thousand to fifty thousand Christian denominations worldwide, and the numbers continue to grow. A good number of these churches desire to be like the early church. Christians want original church worship and they create what they think the church worship was like, but they do not base their church on any historical background. Before 1993 my family began to ask the same questions, What is the church? and, Wouldn't it be nice if the original church still existed? We started looking at the overall church and its history in reverse.

After high school and before going to Westmont College, I spent a year with *Youth with a Mission*, where I was enrolled in their *Discipleship Training School*. There I confirmed what I believed and why I believed it. The DTS consisted of three months in the classroom followed by two months on the mission field putting into practice what we had learned in class. I served in Costa Rica. The next YWAM course was their School of Evangelism, where three months were devoted to apologetics training. Coming from the Greek word *apologia* (speaking in defense of), I learned how to defend my faith, and once again, the class went out to practice what was learned.

Those months were pivotal in my spiritual life, and before college, I knew what I believed, knew why I believed it, and could adequately defend it. Westmont is a Christian college in Santa Barbara, California. Every student at Westmont must take at least four Christian studies courses to graduate. Never the less after my academic study of the Scriptures, historical Christianity, Christian dogma, plus my time at YWAM, I continued with my questions searching for answers to "What is the Church?"

On a rainy day after I finished my year at YWAM; Mom, Dad, and I were discussing Christianity and these topics in particular:

- What became of the apostles?
- Were the New Testament churches founded by various apostles similar in structure and theology throughout Asia Minor?
- Was there uniformity in worship and organization?
- Who were the patristic fathers, and why don't churches everywhere talk about them?
- Was the mother of Jesus, Mary, held in high esteem in the early church? Why in the twenty-first century do few of the Protestant churches breathe a word about Mary until the Christmas season? It seems today as if she's hidden in the attic until December, then placed in a manger scene on somebody's front lawn.

I knew our pastors studied the patristic writers, but why not the parishioners? Dad, Mom, and I wanted continuity not only in our Christian faith but also among fellow believers. Though I'm joking, it feels as if the Lutherans don't like the Catholics, the Baptist dislike the Episcopalians, and none of them could totally agree on doctrine, dogma, or church tradition. This conversation triggered Mom to remember she had been receiving the *Christian Activist: A Journal of Orthodox Opinion*. Much of what we were questioning was being answered in those pages, and the answers revolved around the Orthodox Church. What we found refreshing was whether an Orthodox Church was located in New York City, Cincinnati, Santa Barbara, Athens-Greece, Moscow, Rome, or Jerusalem, the doctrine, theology, dogma and liturgy were the same and had stayed the same since about AD 400.

In the autumn of 1994 I started my freshman year at Westmont College in Santa Barbara. Mom and Dad came to visit, and Mom mentioned there was an Orthodox Church in Isla Vista next to the UCSB. We went. The moment the three of us walked into the church, I felt as if I had been transported into heaven.

Peter Gillquist, the former acquisitions editor for Thomas Nelson books was now a priest at this church. His own book *Becoming Orthodox: A Journey to the Ancient Faith* was a well-researched book that helped my parents and me crystalize our thinking about, and the understanding of, What is the church? and Why Orthodoxy?

Beginning to ask questions on that rainy day about the early church and the people who evangelized, established churches, and faced daunting persecution; started us down the road to our finally embracing and being embraced by the Orthodox Church. We gleaned from Gillquist's *Becoming Orthodox* additional questions that needed to be asked: (1) where did that New Testament Church *go* in history? And (2) How did our own expression of Christianity measure up to the pattern which had been set down in the centuries *following* the Book of Acts?

"Those who don't know history are doomed to repeat it" is true but it is a negatively reinforced view of history. My strong belief, however, that as Christians, we need to know our Christian history with regard to the church. Christian history is not our personal witness. We stand on historical, factual events tracing back nearly two thousand years. We stand on the shoulders of the apostles and martyrs of the church, who were led by the Holy Spirit, who went throughout the known world preaching and teaching, who held to the Scriptures through heresy and persecution, and who established the canon of Scripture in AD 325 at the Council of Nicaea. Those spiritual heroes kept the faith unbroken in the face of persecution and death and laid down the theology, dogma, and liturgical worship, which have been intact and unchanged since the early days after Pentecost.

In taking this living-historical view, one of the questions our family asked was, Would we rather belong to a church that was formed in recent history and its lineage directly linked to its founder from Luther forward, or did we want to belong to the Eastern Byzantine Orthodox Church, whose form and function were unceasingly active since before the time of the emperor Constantine? We thought and still think the choice is a no-brainer. This is a personal choice for any believer, but God will honor your worship of him in any right-believing, Bible-honoring church community.

Gillquist also writes, "Within the Church itself there was a unity of *doctrine* as the apostolic faith was guarded by the great Ecumenical Councils. There was a basic shape or order of the liturgical *worship*. And the *government* of the Church was unified under her five great patriarchal centers—Alexandria, Antioch, Constantinople, Jerusalem, and Rome. Instead of asking if Christian forbears like Justin, Irenaeus, Athanasius, and Chrysostom were in our Church, we began to ask if we were in theirs!"

I believe the crux of Christianity can be summed up by our Lord's virgin birth, death and resurrection, ascension, and the fact Christ was fully human and fully divine. All right-believing orthodox churches espouse this creed, so why was our family so strongly attracted to this ancient Eastern Orthodox church? There are many, many right-believing churches in Atlanta, so why seek out something else, a church so traditional and historical that it traces its founding to the early second century and has not changed substantially in almost two thousand years?

Because of this: the Eastern Church remains the same, but the Western Church has subtly changed over time. Nothing radical all at once, but change it did. The East and West became further separated after Islamic advances and the Crusades. Four hundred sixty-three years after the great schism of AD 1054 between the church in the East and the church in the West, the Protestant Reformation began in the West against the Roman Church, bringing radical change.

The original church in the East continued theologically and organizationally unchanged. The Reformation started a process where now we have twenty-five thousand to fifty thousand Christian denominations vying for their authentic understanding of the original church and Holy Scripture. To apply the earlier attributed quote of Edmund Burke in an Orthodox sense, if we do not know our Christian history, are we not doomed to repeat the failures of schism, thus fragmenting the body of Christ that much more?

So this is where the Lawson family found itself on that rainy day, realizing the church was so different from its origins that it now looked like Plato's "Allegory of the Cave," where the reality people see and think they understand is nothing more than shadows projected on the cave wall from objects passing in front of a fire behind them. I was like that chained person in the cave until I made my way into the sun and saw a greater truth.

We did not become Orthodox overnight or even a year later; it was a slow and educated journey. Friends have asked, "What does it matter what church you go to? Doesn't God work through all Christians?" Our response is an unequivocal *yes*; God does work through all believing churches and denominations. But is this everything that God wanted or intended for us in the first place? If Christ is the head of the church, did God want us to have a divided body? Personally, I want to worship as the early Christians did—and the Orthodox Church continues to do.

What I want you, the reader, to experience is that God loves you and desires that you know the joy of your salvation in whatever community he has you worship. My family would desire for you to delve into the Scriptures and read, digest, and apply what you have learned. I address this to the reader, someone who is in prison or to the person, although not in a physical prison, is perhaps in a psychological prison of manipulation, ego, greed, anger, blaming, gossip, resentment, fear, self-loathing, approval seeking, moral bankruptcy, vanity, self-importance, or so much more. The Orthodox Church believes that we are all sin-sick, the church is a hospital, and the Lord wants us to be healed. Healing comes through the sacraments as well as frequent study implementing biblical principles whereby we begin to break our prison down brick-by-brick and bar-by-bar. The church is here to protect us, keep us accountable, nurture and teach us. It is a place of community where we should belong. Self-study is good and fine, but it does not replace or make up for being embraced within the body of Christ.

We would need the body of Christ for the things we would soon go through.

Chapter 40

# BUSINESS TROUBLE

After September 11, 2001, a series of events combined to turn everything upside down in our business life. Even before 2001, there was the US recession in the late nineties. The recession was noticeable but not as severe as it could have been. Companies reduced their travel budgets and cut their workforces. It was a period to tighten our belts. The horror of 9/11 sent nearly everyone's business into a tailspin. All commercial flights were grounded. There were no reservations coming in; corporations grounded their travelers, and missionaries didn't travel, either.

We were busy, but we were refunding tickets and service fees. Our largest corporate client insisted that we refund all of their service fees which were earned and non-refundable. It was shocking! Stringent security measures were undertaken at all airports, and now it was taking hours to board a flight. Companies no longer flew employees to their regional clients as before. If the trip was less than three hundred miles, they drove.

The internet rose up as a new distribution center for selling airline tickets. Vacation travelers also started using the internet. Our vacation-planning department was coordinating vacations, but clients took our work product and booked the travel themselves. The airlines started cutting commissions, and over a period of several years, airline commissions went from 10 percent to zero when they discontinued them altogether. Now travel agencies had to charge a service fee per transaction to stay in business. Paying for services that were once free turned even more people to the internet. The higher the top, the greater the drop.

We were headed toward being out of business. We had done nothing wrong, and everything was beyond our control. *Now what were we going to do?* Anyone who thinks being a Christian obviates being caught in the crossfire of life needs to reconsider his or her position.

We had started the travel agency business in order provide us with employment and income to pay our bills. Once it got off the ground (pun intended) Harvey and I hoped it might be of interest to Blake as a career direction. Now our firm was in a free fall. Many travel agencies went out of business but thanks be to God we were able to hang on through very difficult times.

When Blake was a junior at Westmont College, one of his courses required an internship with a nearby business, and he worked for Coldwell Banker Realtors in Santa Barbara. He and the firm fell in love with each other, and after his internship Blake passed the California real estate exam. In 1999 Blake graduated from Westmont College with a degree in communication studies and went to work selling real estate full-time in Santa Barbara. But realizing how the town's population comprised either older, very wealthy residents or college and graduate students made him believe it was time to revisit and rethink Atlanta. As much as he loved Santa Barbara, he returned to Atlanta and transferred his real estate license to Georgia.

Even though he was now working full-time selling real estate in Atlanta, Blake turned out to be the "man with the plan." He created a website for us: www. MissionaryAirfareSearch.com, which was the first website with a booking engine for any mission-sending travel agency in the United States. We represented and still do unpublished missionary and humanitarian fares for international travelers, and we worked together to advertise ourselves to every breathing Christian in the United States. In March 2004 Blake joined our travel agency full-time. He was featured in an article that told of his "establishing an enviable success for his family's twenty-five-year old travel company and a classic example of new and innovative ideas replacing old ways of doing business." He was quoted as saying: "I know several people who, like me, have entered their family business and thrived in the environment. As the travel agency business was changing because airlines no longer paid commissions, coupled with people's ability and desire to surf the internet, I told my parents not to fear the internet but rather to embrace it. As many businesses, we had to change with the times."

So here we were, Harvey at age seventy-one and I at seventy-six, and our son was working us to death!

"Now get to work, and make me proud," he'd say to us now and then—a tag line he stole from a very funny TV commercial. There were times Harvey and I thought we'd created a monster.

The years seem to blend together after a while. It's often that Harvey and I remember someone or a past event and find we're talking about something that happened over fifteen years ago. There were times when we felt surrounded by unsolvable problems, yet I can't ever recall when God hasn't been totally faithful. I plead guilty to the times I wanted to serve the Lord—but in an advisory capacity.

During the first year of being a Christian we were sure we had all the answers, but now we realize there is so much we don't know. Have there been times where I didn't hear correctly what I thought God was telling me in my spirit? I don't know. Was I being tested; refined like silver through heat, having the dross skimmed off? I hope so, but I can't say for sure. Have I experienced circumstances where I traveled too fast and got ahead of God? I'm sure I did. Did I always remain still to hear him? Of course not! Then there are other times I thought I heard him, but things didn't seem to work out the way I imagined because of the Lord's "direction." During those times, I tried to determine the lesson I was supposed to learn.

Have I been humbled? Yes, but not entirely. When *Daddy* was published, the publisher booked me on radio and television programs around the country. Some were a great experience. But one option I refused was a book signing in my hometown of Atlanta. I knew myself well enough to know I would note those who didn't come and those who didn't purchase the book if they did attend. That thought process is not the hallmark of a humble person. I've also heard many people remark how an event humbled them. What I heard through my grid system sounded like: "I'm humble and proud of it." Then I've looked around to see the burdens others carry, and I praise God for not having more on my plate than I do.

There have been other times so exceptionally wonderful that I recall Harvey and I pulled to the side of the road to thank God for blessing us so richly and without limit—and requesting that if he intended to bless us further that day would he wait until tomorrow because our hearts were too full to accept any more that day.

Harvey adds: "I definitely feel that Stephen is his most severe critic, and we don't always agree on directions he takes—the book signing for example. But it seems to serve him well in terms of reigning himself in so he doesn't get too far off course. I remember Patty Colson telling me her ministry was to pump Chuck up when he was too deflated and release some air out when he seemed too inflated. Candidly, I feel as though I have the same ministry with my husband as Patty did with hers."

Chapter 41

# STANDING BY BLAKE

Blake has always had a wonderful work ethic. He had jobs during his high school and college years and worked long hours in real estate after graduation. Then, Harvey and I began wondering what was happening when he seemed unable to get up most mornings, and went home early because of exhaustion. His graphic explanation of various aches and severe pain never ended. His knees were killing him. Multiple pains in his back were excruciating. He was unable to fall asleep until five in the morning. The condition progressed until he would be awake for twenty-four to seventy-two hours unable to sleep because of pain. Other times, he would sleep for twenty-four hours straight.

Blake went to every specialist in Atlanta, and each of them gave him medication. He tried diet modifications, chiropractors, herbal medications, and acupuncture treatments. He was tested for everything from Lyme disease to gluten intolerance. He went to Christian healing and deliverance ministries. But the suffering persisted. The closest I was able to relate to his suffering was when I had the Asian flu in my early twenties. I recall lying in bed unable to move. There wasn't a place on my body that didn't ache. All I could do was sleep, and I would wake up in a pool of perspiration from my fever. I was reliving the experience with Blake, but unlike an Asian flu that runs its course, Blake continued in agony. Blake's short-term memory was failing him. He always looked glassy-eyed. His responses to any questions were becoming lengthy and tedious. His thought process appeared slow. Finally, Blake visited the rheumatology department at Emory University Clinic. He was diagnosed with chronic fatigue and fibromyalgia, a disease syndrome, with no known cure, that affects a person's soft tissues and brings terrible pain as well as exhaustion.

From the first day we realized Blake had a problem, he became the object of soaking prayer by Harvey and me and many prayer groups in Atlanta. Weeks, months, and years passed with no improvement. If he were not working for family, he would be considered totally unemployable. The travel business is an industry where mistakes are very expensive to correct. There came a time when even we were no longer able to employ him. He lost any social life. He would talk with people on the phone and make plans only to find he slept through them.

What was the spiritual significance to this? Were the sins of the father transferred to the son? Scripture assured Harvey and me that if there were any such link, it had been broken in Christ. We continued in prayer, and I cried out to God to heal Blake by allowing me to be his burden bearer. Surely God would understand the concept better than anyone.

Harvey recalls, "Words can't express what it's like to see your child suffer this way without, short of a miracle, any hope of recovery. Only those who live it are able to have any concept. Fibromyalgia afflicts women ninety-five percent of the time. It's said that when it happens to a man, it comes with a greater force. If all this weren't discouraging enough, everyone knew of someone in a new cottage industry selling snake oil for fibromyalgia. In fall 2012 Blake spent a month at the Mayo Clinic Pain Rehab Center in Jacksonville, Florida, where he went through additional testing and learned behavior modification that allows him to live with a much greater purpose. The pain still exists, and minus direct intervention by the Lord, he will continue to have this thorn in the flesh. In the final analysis, it's up to God. Blake is of the opinion he is in the middle of research for his own book, and he may be right. His is a great testimony, and I'm as proud of him as it's possible to be."

I went to prison knowing in my heart that God wasn't a trickster and would be faithful in all things. He was faithful during my time in prison and faithful with Harvey and Blake serving a harsh sentence at home in Atlanta. Now thirty-four years later, I can't recall a time God wasn't trustworthy or faithful. This doesn't mean our timetables were always in sync. I've always loved the times he said yes. I sometimes hated when the answer was no, and I grew frustrated when the answer was *Wait a while*. However, even during those times, I knew he was aware of my feelings of "hope deferred makes the heart sick." I knew it when I went to prison at forty-two and I'm sure of it now decades later.

# Chapter 42

# THE END OF THE BEGINNING

If you are a Christian and this book has brought someone to mind, please send it to them because so many are in prisons of their own making.

If you have not asked Christ into your life, I pray that our opening our lives to you has been of value and been thought provoking. If you have never considered a personal relationship with the Lord, perhaps now would be a good time to give it some thought.

Whatever your impression of organized religion, pretend to place it on a slab in the morgue and roll it into the wall. Whatever your thoughts are about Christians being weak, phonies, or hypocrites, likewise, put it on another slab and roll it into the wall. Other people's issues have nothing to do with you! In any event, they hold no legitimacy, pro or con, regarding the valid reality of God. Perhaps at some future time you might like to return to the morgue, roll out the corpse, and examine it again. It makes for a good intellectual exercise. But for now, let's concern ourselves only with you.

It isn't by chance you are reading this book. It's a divine appointment, and your life is about to change forever. Faith is free, and you don't need much of it to begin—maybe just the size of a grain of salt or a mustard seed in the hope I'm right and there really is help. But as your car won't start until you activate the ignition, nothing will happen unless you sincerely invite the Lord into your heart. You can sit there until the next snowfall hits your area, but the car still won't start unless you are proactive. Further, you cannot sit in church all Sunday and become a Christian any more than you're able to sit in your garage and become a Mercedes. You can purchase an expensive Italian-designed suit along with a shirt and tie—but you're still going to be the same person on the inside, and that's where the change needs to begin, from the inside out.

First off, tell God you are willing to give him a chance. Read the following to yourself, and if you agree, read it aloud.

> God, I really have no idea if what I'm reading can possibly be true. If it is, I want in my life what has been written on these pages, because I'm tired of going it alone. Only you and I are aware of everything I have ever done, and every thought I have ever had. Maybe that's why I've continued to run away. I've been scared of you, Lord, because I never believed I could be forgiven. More than anything, I want the gift of peace. In the best way I know how, I pray that Jesus Christ will come into my heart to forgive and remake me. I've tried it my way too long, and I pray this simple prayer in the hope you will hear me and

show your love and caring for me. Demonstrate to me through a small, personal miracle that lets me know you've heard me. I'm opening the door to my heart and invite you in. Come, Lord Jesus. Amen.

Our prayer for you:

Father, you know the reader of this book intimately because you are the one who knit this person together in his or her mother's womb and loved this person before the foundation of time. Take the expressions found on these pages and apply them to this reader's heart in a way he or she will understand it to be a miracle—especially for this person. Let this reader know he or she is forgiven and the slate is wiped clean. Provide your peace beyond all understanding regardless of circumstances. Not as the world offers peace but only as you can offer. Also, as a newborn baby hungers for mother's milk, give this newborn in Christ a hunger for your Word. Thank you for the gift of salvation but also the knowledge we no longer have to go through life alone. Thank you for your ever-present help, which allows us to see through different eyes and hear through different ears and make righteous decisions with comfort. Thank you for forgiving all his or her past sins. I pray for the person holding this book, in the name of the Father, Son, and Holy Spirit. Amen.

Stephen passed away in April 2015, and here we include

his obituary, his final witness:

In Memory of Stephen P. Lawson
May 24, 1937–April 23, 2015

Stephen P. Lawson of Smyrna, Georgia, died Thursday, April 23, of complications from colon and liver cancer. Rather than offering a standard obituary of accomplishments, Stephen chose to write the following:

> By the time you read this, my ongoing process of sanctification has been short-circuited by death, no doubt an ailment my gastroenterologist would consider life-threatening. My belief is that I have asked forgiveness of everyone I have either wronged or offended as I have attempted to live out my last years in peace and repentance. I correctly made the two wisest decisions of my life: the person I was to spend my life with here on earth, Elyse Harvey Reinhard Lawson, and the person I was to spend eternity with after I died, Jesus Christ. In the former, I married my best friend and the nicest person I ever knew. We were married for forty-eight years. Blake Stiles Lawson is our son and a person of great integrity. My greatest honor in life was being Harvey's husband and Blake's dad. I have lived a wonderful life and truly want for nothing. I experienced the Lord in the middle of my circumstances, and he was faithful to work all things together for the good for those who love him and are called according to his purposes. His mercy endures forever, and I can depend on his saving grace. I have

been blessed beyond measure. Now I join the cloud of witnesses who have preceded me in proclaiming: "Glory to the Father, Son and the Holy Spirit, now and ever unto the ages of ages. Amen. "

Born in New York City on May 24, 1937, to Lillian Pollack Lawson and Sanford Everett Lawson he was preceded in death by his parents and sister, Rosemary L. Strickman. He attended Kentucky Military Institute and graduated from the Franklin School in New York City. He was awarded a basketball scholarship to New York University, a Division 1 school at the time, and played his freshman and sophomore years before seriously injuring his knee. Married in 1966 to the former Elyse Harvey Reinhard of Atlanta, they settled in Atlanta. After several life-changing events, Mr. Lawson authored a bestselling Christian book, *Daddy, Why Are You Going to Jail?* released by Harold Shaw Publishers in 1992. The book was updated in 2014. Additionally he authored several novels: *The Arrangement* and *The Fix* as well as two non-fiction books: *Obama: He Reminds Me of the Person I Used to Be* and *Schmucks and Other White Collar Criminals.* All books are available as ebooks on Amazon.

Funeral services will be held on Wednesday, April 29, at 10:30 a.m. at Holy Transfiguration Greek Orthodox Church, 3431 Trickum Road, Marietta, Georgia 30066. In lieu of flowers, donations can be made to Reflections Ministries, Inc. in Atlanta and the Orthodox Christian Mission Center located in St. Augustine, Florida.

It has been our desire to demonstrate to you the faithfulness, mercy, and love of God and to finish the race with determination, endurance, and perseverance. Stephen finished his race with joy and anticipation of being with the Lord. Although Blake and I miss him terribly, we have total peace and know we are separated for only a season of time. I often say with a smile that Stephen is just out of cell phone range!

# Chapter 43

# LAST WORD FROM HARVEY

A s Stephen, Blake, and I left behind the evangelical church to enter the historical church of the early Christians, our Orthodox friends and clergy could comment that we write and sound like Protestant evangelicals to this day. And they would not be wrong.

Stephen and I always have had a heart for evangelism and would say, "I tell you, now is the time of God's favor, now is the day of salvation" (2 Corinthians 6:2). Dear friend, what are you waiting for? Our book is written to the person who perhaps is unchurched, or one who attended church earlier but became disenchanted, or one who only attends on Christmas and Easter and has no idea of the richness of Scripture, or how much they are loved by God; or perhaps one who is "backslidden," a term sounding more evangelical than Orthodox. However, whether Orthodox, Roman Catholic, or Protestant, God's love for each of us knows no boundaries of where we line up in the faith. God's concern for each of us is that we are in Christ. We are to know him and to make him known to others.

It may surprise some to learn the Orthodox Church was the first to evangelize throughout the world. Historically, they spread the faith through Asia Minor, Northern Africa, and Europe during the patristic and medieval periods. They were hard core as they risked their lives and endured persecution and martyrdom for spreading the Christian faith for the first three hundred years. In AD 313 the emperor of Rome, Constantine the Great, became a Christian, and he granted Christians freedom of worship. When the Byzantine missionaries, notably Saints Cyril and Methodius, began converting the Slavic people, they knew the best missionary method was to teach, preach, and worship in the familiar local language. They went about translating Scripture, worship services, and prayers into local languages.

The fourth through the tenth centuries were noteworthy for the internal and external development of the church. Through the ecumenical councils, the New Testament was determined. The churches in the five great ecclesiastical centers used the same liturgy in the worship services. The "Fathers of the Church" developed the theology. It all happened during this time frame, yet we twenty-first-century Christians have little awareness of the persecution, effort, and price paid by those believers. Unless one had come upon the history of the Russian Church, most American Christians would be unaware that Russia discovered and adopted the Orthodox Church around AD 1000.

The Byzantine Empire was constantly on guard against the neighboring Persians and Muslims. Once Muslims overtook a country, limitations were imposed upon the church, especially as it pertained to evangelism. When

Muslims conquered Constantinople (present-day Istanbul), the seat of the Eastern Church, in 1453, the Byzantine Empire came to an end, and vast lands of Asia Minor fell subject to non-Christians. The great ecclesiastical cities of Alexandria, Antioch, and Jerusalem had been under the political control of Islam centuries earlier, and now Constantinople, the capital, had been conquered. Throughout the Ottoman Empire, Christians were treated as second-class citizens and paid heavy taxes for the privilege of staying alive. Yet thousands of Christians suffered martyrdom; bishops were murdered; Christian schools, churches and monasteries were closed and destroyed. Proselytizing by Christians was forbidden. Conversions went only one way—to Islam.

When Orthodox believers began immigrating to the United States from Greece, Asia Minor, Eastern Europe, Russia, Lebanon, and Syria, their desire was to become good Americans—learn English, get a job, and do well. But they also established Orthodox churches, which became places of security and comfort where they shared a common language from home with people of similar experience, language, and culture. Since the time Muslims conquered Asia Minor, evangelism had been successfully repressed through persecution and martyrdom. Thus evangelism as Orthodoxy historically knew it lost its priority due to the people's desire to survive.

Given this history, I would venture to say that many American Orthodox believers find evangelical vocabulary quizzical. They aren't quite sure what is meant by "ask Jesus into your heart" or being "born again." Orthodox believers come into the faith and into the church at baptism and chrismation. When a person is baptized and chrismated, they receive Christ, renounce Satan, ask for forgiveness of sins, and receive the Holy Spirit. The Orthodox way of receiving Christ and becoming a Christian is more formal, and the process includes taking a vow before the Lord. It is a lengthy service that follows the ancient creeds and liturgy and covers all the spiritual bases—nothing is left out. The catechumen studies for a minimum of a year before he or she comes into the church as a member to receive the sacraments and worship fully. None of this is taken lightly.

The Protestant evangelical believes that "today is the day of salvation," and someone should pray with the unbeliever then and there and help them come into the kingdom of God. Once a person prays to receive Christ, renounce Satan, and ask God for forgiveness of sins, they are pointed toward a Bible-believing church and good teaching for discipleship.

Both traditions want the same outcome for the unbeliever: that they should become a faithful follower of Christ. Both Orthodox and Protestant would insist upon baptism for the new believer. But the process is different. For the Orthodox, the priest encourages and prepares the catechumen for life in Christ and for the service of baptism and chrismation. The Protestant believer commonly has someone from the laity pray with them to receive Christ and lead them to a good church to meet with a pastor and prepare to be baptized.

If a theologian were writing this, he or she would probably take exception to my simplistic explanation.

Regardless, it is always best to speak with a pastor or priest regarding your spiritual life and where you hope to spend eternity. Take classes, and invest yourself in the best teaching and worship services. Find a Christian community, and learn about this wonderful God and his plan for your life.

I hope this historical perspective is helpful toward understanding Orthodoxy. Beyond that, whatever tradition we call home, whether a canonical Orthodox Church, a Bible believing nondenominational church, a mainline denominational church, or the Roman Catholic Church, our mutual goal should be to bring those who do not have a connection with Christ into a meaningful personal relationship with Him.

In conclusion, Stephen would agree with me that prison or a life-crisis can truly be a blessing if we will allow God to work through it. For us prison was the gift of perspective. Without the hardship of prison and the life-changing consequences, we shudder to think how our lives could have ended up if we had continued on a path of too much financial success. John Newton, author of *"Amazing Grace,"* after he gave up the slave trade once said, "I have reason to praise God for my trials, for most probably I should have been ruined without them." Aleksandr Solzhenitsyn, author of *The Gulag Archipelago,* suffered twenty years in Russian prisons but wrote in that book, "Bless you prison, bless you for being in my life. For there, lying upon the rotting prison straw, I came to realize that the object of life is not prosperity as we are made to believe, but the maturity of the human soul."

While Stephen was in prison, I clung to the Scripture found in Jeremiah 29:11, "'For I know the plans I have for you,' declares the LORD, 'plans to prosper you and not to harm you, plans to give you hope and a future.'" The Lord was faithful, and he gave us a future and a hope. Not only that, he walked with us in the midst of the crisis of prison and continued to see us through the rough places once released. Stephen never lost sight of the remarkable journey that only God could map out. He never forgot that once he worked in a downtown parking lot, and then God allowed us to build a successful travel business. We never recovered the financial success as we once knew it, but we gained two things of much greater value—peace that passes all understanding and a "maturity of the soul."

If you have asked Christ into your life and are courageous enough to believe God no matter if circumstances indicate otherwise, I know he will bless you abundantly in much the manner he has with us.

If you feel led to contact us, please feel free to do so. If by letter: P.O. Box 724377, Atlanta, GA 31139. We will attempt to answer everyone. My email address is: info@daddybook. org. If Blake and I are able to be of encouragement to anyone or any congregation, we will consider it a blessing. We are available for speaking engagements at churches or church conferences.

Finally, please know that monies earned from the sale of this book or donations are given to Angel Tree, a Prison Fellowship ministry, and Orthodox Christian Prison Ministry. A 501(c)(3) non-profit corporation has been established to accept book sales and donations for ministry. Books can be purchased directly on our website daddybook. org or on Amazon.com.

# APPENDIX 1

I f you are interested in the Greek Orthodox Chrismation service, a complete version may be found online at *www.goarch.org/-/the-service-of-holy-bapti-1*. I would encourage you to attend a Canonical Orthodox church service in your city. The Sunday morning service is the same at any Orthodox church in the world, using the liturgy of St. John Chrysostom c. 347-407. He was bishop in Syria and the Archbishop of Constantinople. The service for an adult convert who has been previously baptized is slightly different than the service for an infant.

The liturgical texts including the Divine Liturgy, Matins, Vespers, Sacraments, Memorials and Funerals as well as Occasional Services including the Akathist Hymn, which is sung on Friday nights during Lent can be found at the following URL: www.goarch.org/chapel/texts.

I am in no way suggesting conversion to Orthodoxy, but I am offering this information as a way for you to have a deeper understanding of the history of our glorious Christian faith by attending a service that is repeated in thousands of churches around the world every week. The service will be in a local language but the liturgy of St. John Chrysostom is followed in every Orthodox Church whether it is Greek, Antiochian, Russian or any Canonical Orthodox Church in the world.

# APPENDIX 2

f you are interested in Eastern Orthodoxy, we recommend any of the following books:

- *The Orthodox Church* by Timothy Ware (aka Bishop Kallistos Ware)
- *The Orthodox Way* by Bishop Kallistos Ware
- *Introducing the Orthodox Church: Its Faith and Life* by Anthony M. Coniaris
- *Becoming Orthodox: A Journey to the Ancient Christian Faith* by Peter Gillquist
- *Facing East* by Frederica Matthews-Green
- *The Faith, Understanding Orthodox Christianity* by Clark Carlton
- *For the Life of the World* by Alexander Schmemann
- *Of Water and The Spirit, A Liturgical Study of Baptism* by Alexander Schmemann

Also to name but a few non-Orthodox writers from whom we benefited greatly prior to becoming Orthodox and continue to read:

- *The Knowledge of the Holy* and *The Pursuit of God* by A. W. Tozer

  Although Tozer was not Eastern Orthodox, his writings were as orthodox as any Protestant writer of the twentieth century.

- *Conformed to His Image: Biblical and Practical Approaches to Spiritual Formation* by Kenneth Boa

- *Life in the Presence of God: Practices for Living in the Light of Eternity by* Kenneth Boa

- KenBoa.org, is filled with wonderful teaching and ministry aids

- All books by C.S. Lewis: *Mere Christianity,* The Narnia Series for children and adults, The Space Trilogy, *The Great Divorce, The Screwtape Letters, Miracles, Surprised by Joy,* to name but a very few

- *The Divine Conspiracy* by Dallas Willard

The list could continue on and on as I look at the wonderful books in our collection, but we have been deeply blessed by all of the above authors.